# What People Are Saying About

# Justice, Love, and Organizational Healing

How can consulting be a practice for internal and collective transformation? How does one consult from a place of love? With wisdom born from decades of experience, Ora Grodsky gives us a brilliant and powerful handbook — complete with practical tools and powerful stories — on how organizations can lead with courage, clarity, and imagination. A must-have guide for all consultants and leaders committed to building a world of love and justice!

**Valarie Kaur,** author of *See No Stranger* and founder of the Revolutionary Love Project.

As a young man, I distrusted most organizations. However noble their mission statements, most seemed driven by self-interest, self-promotion, and self-protection. So when I first heard people talk about the power of love to transform organizational life, I was a skeptic. But as I came to know the work of people like Ora Grodsky — people who bring intelligence, compassion, long experience and proven practices to the table — my skepticism was replaced by hope for the future. At a time when institutional distrust is unraveling the fabric of democracy itself, we need that hope. I know of no better book than *Justice, Love, and Organizational Healing* to energize, edify and guide anyone who cares about the integrity of the organizations on which we depend.

**Parker J. Palmer**, author of *A Hidden Wholeness, Let Your Life Speak,* and *The Courage to Teach.*

An amazing piece of work! A gift to consultants of all stripes — one that will enrich their practice...and their lives. Wise, informative, practical, generous, humble, and provocative; a challenge to ground one's practice in the values one professes to hold dear. In Ora Grodsky's case, this translates into the primacy of Love and Justice in her work and life.
**Barry Oshry,** author of *Seeing Systems.*

Ora Grodsky has seized the time and honed the written word to deliver and share the depth of her life experience and heart. This compilation of life's work, her book is a guide to building upon and enhancing a pillar of justice...the pillar of love. Ora guides us away from the vortex of the inauthentic fad of consulting... into the light of life practice and service leadership built on a foundation of love. While never leaving out the gift of self-healing into love...as a prerequisite for being love's conduit.
**Joyce Shabazz,** Anti-racism consultant, Evolutions, LLC.

*Justice, Love, and Organizational Healing: A Guide to Transformational Consulting* is both inspirational and eminently practical — not only "how to" but "why to." Profound concepts like love and justice are skillfully integrated with everything from how to structure a consulting engagement to dealing with resistance and setting fees. Equally valuable to consultants, leaders and all those interested in transforming organizations.
**Robert Gass, Ed.D.,** Founder of the Rockwood Leadership Institute.

# Justice, Love, and Organizational Healing

## A Guide to Transformational Consulting

# Justice, Love, and Organizational Healing

## A Guide to Transformational Consulting

Ora C. Grodsky

**BUSINESS BOOKS**

London, UK
Washington, DC, USA

## CollectiveInk

First published by Business Books, 2025
Business Books is an imprint of Collective Ink Ltd.,
Unit 11, Shepperton House, 89 Shepperton Road, London, N1 3DF
office@collectiveink.com
www.collectiveinkbooks.com
www.collectiveinkbooks.com/business-books/

For distributor details and how to order please visit the 'Ordering' section on our website.

Text copyright: Ora C. Grodsky 2023

ISBN: 978 1 80341 699 1
978 1 80341 725 7 (ebook)
Library of Congress Control Number: 2023950037

A CIP catalogue record for this book is available from the British Library.

Design: Lapiz Digital Services

UK: Printed and bound by CPI Group (UK) Ltd, Croydon, CR0 4YY
Printed in North America by CPI GPS partners

We operate a distinctive and ethical publishing philosophy in all areas of our business, from our global network of authors to production and worldwide distribution.

# Table of Contents

| | |
|---|---|
| Acknowledgements | xiii |
| Introduction | xv |
| Overview | xxi |
| **1. What Is a Transformational Consultant?** | 1 |
| Types of Consulting | 3 |
| Consulting Offers | 6 |
| Consulting Rhythms | 8 |
| Consultant Postures | 11 |
| Rooting in Ourselves | 13 |
| My Experience as a White Consultant | 15 |
| **2. The Business of Practice** | 20 |
| Building a Practice | 21 |
| Colleagues and Collaborators | 23 |
| Selecting Clients | 25 |
| Contract with Care | 31 |
| Setting Fees | 37 |
| When the Work Is Done | 39 |
| **3. Beginning an Engagement** | 41 |
| Who Is the Client? | 42 |
| Articulate the Process | 43 |
| Assemble Champions | 46 |
| Discovery and Assessment | 49 |
| **4. We Shape Systems as Systems Shape Us** | 58 |
| Racism and Systemic Oppression | 58 |
| Mental Models and Mistaken Facticity | 60 |
| Power | 64 |
| Culture | 70 |
| **5. Levers of Change** | 76 |
| Careful Pacing | 77 |
| Develop and Support Leadership | 79 |
| Tell the Truth | 86 |

Practice Accountability    90

Clarify Guiding Ideas    96

Imagine and Plan for the Future    103

A Story of Transformational Change    111

6. **Transformational Change Is Hard Work**    116

Conflict with Care    117

Anticipate Resistance    125

Discomfort and Uncertainty    130

Overwhelm and Urgency    135

When to Act and When to Pause    143

7. **Creating Meaningful Meetings**    148

Alignment    149

Pre-Meeting Planning    151

Agendas    156

Shifting the Plan    159

Space    163

Accessibility    166

Attending to Equity    168

Decision-Making    171

8. **Facilitating: Holding Space**    180

Trust    183

Essential Facilitation Skills: Listening, Asking
Questions, Reflecting, and Synthesizing    184

Presence and Vulnerability    189

Who Facilitates?    194

The Inside Job    195

**Conclusion**    199

**Appendix: Tools and Resources**    200

Tools and Resources for Planning    202

POP    202

Strategic Moments: What to do
when you don't know what to do...    203

Strategy Filter    206

Tools and Resources for Navigating Conflict 207
    The Conflict Avoidance Escalator 207
    Non-Violent Communication (NVC) 209
    DiSC 210
Tools and Resources for Meetings and
    Decision-Making 210
    Check-ins (and Check-outs) 210
    Meeting Guidelines 213
    Meeting Evaluations 215
    Circle Process 216
    Fist to Five and Thumb Polls 216
    Deep Democracy 217
    Decision Matrix 218
Tools and Resources for Navigating Change 220
    The Wheel of Change 220
    Appreciative Inquiry 222
    Immunity to Change 223
Tools and Resources for Understanding Systems 225
    Organizational and Team Assessment Tools 225
    Seeing Systems 228
    Organizational Ecosystems 231

In loving memory of my parents, Phyllis Grodsky
and David Grodsky, and my mentor and friend
Steven Brion-Meisels. Wherever you are,
I hope this book makes you smile.

# Acknowledgements

Let me begin with profound gratitude for my clients, whose dedication to building a more just and loving world, and the gift of our work together, is the foundation of this book.

This book and I stand on the shoulders of countless practitioners, thinkers, educators, leaders, and authors. I am incredibly appreciative of everyone who has come before me and has traveled alongside me, lighting the path. I have done my best to credit the people behind the ideas and practices that inform my thinking. It is my hope that readers will continue to acknowledge the original sources of the wisdom they glean from these pages.

I was blessed with enormous love, support, encouragement, and help throughout my writing journey. Many friends, colleagues, and family members spent countless hours discussing ideas with me, providing valuable feedback, and gently pushing me when I needed it. My heartfelt thanks to each of you for sharing your time, wisdom, and care, Amanda Silver, Andy Kirshner, Anne Litwin, April Brumson, Avia Moore, Betty Burkes, Cathy Hoffman, Christine Williams, Cindy Carpenter, Claudia Lach, Chrysta Wilson, Dana Kennedy, Rabbi David Jaffe, Isaac Grody-Patinkin, Janet Penn, Jen Kiok, Joe Sammen, Joe Curnow, Julia Riseman, Kate Engle, Kathleen Engel, Laurie Goldman, Liz Aeschlimann, Maxine Hart, Megan Madison, Melody Brazo, Miriam Messinger, Orah Fireman, Paul Behrman, Seth Kirshenbaum, Shaya French, Stephanie Rowden, Tara Edelschick, and Wendy Krom.

I want to extend a special shout-out to my dear colleagues in my consultants' group: Joyce Shabazz, Jeremy Phillips, Daniel Michaud Weinstock, and Melinda Barbosa. Your partnership in learning and practice is a great blessing. My work, my personhood, and this book would not be what they are without you.

I am grateful to everyone who generously provided beautiful spaces for me to write and think while working on the book: the Grody-Patinkin family, Open Meadow Zen Center, the Cochran family, the Engel-Rebitzer family, the Khitrik family, and the Levine Rosenthal family, and for Robin Bernstein, whose pomodoros gave me rocket fuel.

My deep appreciation to my dear friend Andrea Schwartz-Feit for allowing her beautiful painting to grace the cover. Special thanks to Haley McDevitt for the wonderful illustrations, to Alex Thorne, Cora Kircher, Alan Hunter, and Sami Grover for their invaluable guidance and support on the journey to publication, and to Benita Danzing for jumping in at the finish line.

This book would not have been possible without my editor, Rebecca Steinitz. Her ability to turn rambling language into engaging text is a wonder. It is a gift to me and to everyone who will read this book.

Finally, words alone cannot adequately express my gratitude for my wonderful husband, Jonathan Rosenthal, and our incredible daughters, Sasha Grodsky and Zoe Grodsky. Every day, I am inspired and sustained by their steadfast love. This book simply would not exist without their insightful feedback and loving support.

# Introduction

*The moment we choose to love we begin to move against domination, against oppression. The moment we choose to love we begin to move towards freedom, to act in ways that liberate ourselves and others.*

— bell hooks

*We must act as if our institutions are ours to create, our learning is ours to define, our leadership we seek is ours to become.*

— Peter Block

When I was first consulting, a friend asked me what I did. "I bring out love in organizations and help them become more effective," I said, trying on the idea. "What?" she replied, incredulous and maybe even a little disdainful. The unspoken message was loud and clear. I was in la-la land — ungrounded at best and perhaps even dangerously foolish. I didn't talk about love in my work for years after that.

Today, thanks to the courageous and brilliant work of bell hooks, Valarie Kaur, and the many others who have lifted up the critical role of love in the struggle for justice, such conversations are no longer taboo. The relational connections that can move human hearts and our care for each other are no longer afterthoughts. Love is foundational as we seek to heal a broken world.

The systems we've created by acting without love and regard for life have formed the perilous circumstances in which we find ourselves now: entrenched oppression, catastrophic human displacement, climate disaster, and endangered democracy. In order to heal, we need solutions grounded in love for humanity and care for our planet. To create these solutions, we need to radically change our beliefs and behaviors about how we live together on this planet.

Yet every organization and movement working for a just and sustainable world is made up of human beings with individual and collective challenges. We stumble over ourselves and each other, try to do the best we can, forget to hold one another with grace, and succumb to the pressures and urgency of the world. No matter how hard we try, it can be difficult to resist the messages of racism, patriarchy, and capitalism loudly proclaiming that dominance and subjugation are inevitable and we must claim our share at the expense of others.

But despite all the evidence to the contrary, we are capable of great love as a species and as individuals. Throughout human history, people have figured out that there is another way to live our lives: we can simultaneously tend to our own well-being, the well-being of others, and the health of our environment. Now, more than ever, we must resist the urgency and competition that surrounds us and ground our work in our hopes. In order to build the world we want, we need to build new skills, ways of being, and habits in ourselves, our organizations, and our movements.

*Justice, Love, and Organizational Healing* is about transformational consulting grounded in the infinite task of reaching for truth and returning to love that calls forth systemic and individual change. It offers guidance for consultants working to help individuals and organizations be more effective in their work for justice. In it, you'll find consulting postures, mindsets, practices, and tools that facilitate integrity and alignment between our inner selves, our organizations, how we work together, and our efforts to bring about a just and sustainable world.

Over the 25+ years I've been a consultant, I've had the honor of working with thousands of people in more than 200 organizations. I have facilitated and co-facilitated hundreds of planning, change, team development, conflict resolution, racial justice, and leadership development processes, not to mention countless meetings.

I found my way to organizational development after experiencing both the miracle and misery of working inside an organization I loved, an organization that really mattered and made a difference. I knew both the magnificence of flow, the glorious feeling of working in alignment with others to create something beautiful, and the pain and frustration of failure — to get our shit together, create what we knew could be, walk the talk of our values and aspirations, and treat each other well when things got tough.

"This can't be all that's possible," my younger self thought. "How can we humans work together to create a just and sustainable world while nourishing and sustaining our own lives and spirits?" This question led me back to graduate school and onto the path of organizational development. It has guided my life and work for over a quarter of a century.

I never imagined I would be an independent consultant, and it certainly wasn't what I set out to do long term. From my prior professional experiences (providing training and technical assistance for public health efforts; teaching and practicing acupuncture; co-founding a holistic public health clinic; and holding leadership roles in non-profits and a school), I knew that I loved facilitating learning, growth, and healing and had a passionate curiosity about the workings of organizations and groups. But I did not see myself as someone who would thrive in an environment of constant uncertainty and change, so consulting was not an obvious choice.

Like many consultants, I found myself stepping into the role after leaving a job without a new one in hand. "What will you do next?" people asked. "I'll be consulting," I said, often not saying the truth that was also present: "I'll be sitting in the abyss, figuring out my next steps."

The week I left what turned out to be my last 9-5 job, I was offered two relatively big and stable consulting contracts. I thought I might freelance for a year or two as a temporary perch while I had two young kids at home. To my surprise, consulting and I took to each other well. Coming in from the outside, holding sacred space for people to grow, and accompanying, guiding, and helping them to be accountable to their aspirations became my vocation, passion, and calling. And it has been a long road with many lessons hard learned.

I am awed by the generous people I have worked with and the lessons I have learned from countless colleagues, mentors, clients, authors, thinkers, and friends. I have built much of my understanding about consulting from the ideas they exposed me to, which I have put together in my own way through the lens of my identity as a cis-gendered, straight, white, formally educated, middle-aged, typically abled, economically resourced woman.

In addition to extensive study of organizational development, I trace the roots of my approach to long-standing traditions I have embraced to find meaning and make sense of this complex world. These include a commitment to racial, social, gender, environmental, and economic justice from my Ashkenazi Jewish heritage and an embodied understanding of energy and healing imbued by my early training and practice in Traditional Chinese Medicine (TCM).

Two other critical influences have been crucial to the development of my approach over the years. One is the organizational development methodologies I first encountered in graduate school and continued to study. Many of these processes for authentic dialogue and collaboration, tools for understanding and shifting systems, and leadership development practices grounded in vulnerability and self-knowledge foster genuine human connection and democratization of voice. The other is my growing understanding, over the last many years, of how deeply the impact of racism and dominance is baked into the DNA of most, if not all, systems in the US — and into myself. I deeply appreciate the generosity of friends, colleagues, teachers, public thinkers, and others whose wisdom, insights, and experiences have led me to this understanding.

This awareness has caused me to question the organizational development canon, which was largely developed by white men working inside extractive corporations. Despite all I have learned from that canon and how helpful it has been to my work, its origin and the ways it has been used to grease the wheels of capitalism and white dominance left me increasingly unsettled. The incongruities made me hear Audre Lorde's wisdom: "the master's tools will never dismantle the master's house."

I've been wrestling with this dilemma for a long time; in one of our many luminous conversations, my dear mentor, friend, and frequent consulting partner, Joyce Shabazz, helped me come to a good understanding. Joyce pointed out that most of these tools and processes are not new. In fact, many are rooted in long-time wisdom from varied cultures that were never formally codified. "We should utilize these tools because they are in the world," Joyce said, "but let's be clear about who has had access to concretizing and claiming them and who hasn't."

The strategy I have used here is both to present these tools and resources in the context of my experiences with them and to place them alongside tools and resources developed within contexts of liberation, some by me, some by colleagues and other leaders and organizational development professionals. It is my hope that this will make it easier to use them in the service of justice.

You may have noticed me refer above to *white dominance*. I want to say a word about why I use this term when the common phrase these days is *white supremacy*. Several years ago, I saw the rapper, KRS-One, give a talk. His powerful words and sharp analysis of racism in the US were piercing. Among many other pearls of wisdom, he said, "Why do we call it white supremacy? Supreme means something really good! There's nothing good about 'white supremacy." I learned from Joyce Shabazz to use the term dominance instead, which accurately describes where we are: one group of people attempting to control and take power from another. I still refer to white supremacy ideology and culture when they can be useful descriptors.

I can only imagine the faint outlines of how the field of organizational development will change in years to come — and how we will change how we organize ourselves to do work. What I offer in this book comes from what I know and am continuing to learn at this moment in time. I'm sharing my gathered wisdom and experience with the hope that it will be a useful resource to anyone who also feels a call to help organizations be and do better as an expression of justice, care, and love and that it can contribute to a foundation for future exploration and development.

*Do not be daunted by the enormity of the world's grief. Do justly now, love mercy now, walk humbly now. You are not obligated to complete the work, but neither are you free to abandon it.*
– Micah 6:8; Pirkei Avot 2:16.

# Overview

The book follows the arc of a consulting engagement. It begins with an introduction to consulting as a practice, moves on to setting up and starting an engagement, and then addresses the work's actions, phases, challenges, and approaches. You can read it from beginning to end or dive straight into relevant sections.

Each chapter explores the theoretical and tangible aspects of consulting, including the philosophical underpinnings of my approach and logistical "how-tos." Throughout the book, I include exemplary stories that show how I put my values and approaches into practice. I fictionalized these stories on the basis of my experiences, so I could give detail, color, and texture to the lessons they bear while protecting client confidentiality. Many chapters also include what my beloved late mentor, Steven Brion-Meisels, called our "come from" place: the inner work and attitudes that are central to skillful transformational consulting.

Throughout the book, I talk extensively about "systems," by which most obviously I mean organizations and institutions: schools, places of worship, communities, and governments. However, any place humans come together in an organized way is also a system, and the insights the book offers can also apply to families, friend groups, online communities, etc.

In the appendix, I present the tools and resources I find most essential to my practice along with examples of how I use them.

Chapter 1, *What is a Transformational Consultant?* explores the nature of transformational consulting and what it means to consult from a place of love. It considers different types of consulting and consulting offers, the rhythms of consulting and life as a consultant, my experience of being a white consultant committed to racial justice, and the internal spiritual aspects of being a consultant.

Chapter 2, *The Business of Practice*, presents the elements of building and maintaining a consulting practice and forming trusted consulting relationships, including marketing, selecting clients, setting fees, contracting, and completing engagements. If this chapter sounds dry and you are tempted to skip it, please don't. If you are consulting or considering consulting, it's chock-full of important ideas and information that are essential to running a successful consulting practice.

Chapter 3, *Beginning an Engagement*, considers the early stages of consulting engagements — how to enter and learn about the condition of an organizational system in ways that build trust and enhance the work you and your client will do together. This includes conducting assessments, process mapping, and assembling groups to guide and champion the work.

Chapter 4, *We Shape Systems as Systems Shape Us*, explores what the powerful forces that shape our lives and society can look like inside organizations. Consultants need to understand these forces, including the ubiquitous toxicity of racism and systemic oppression, and how they show up in our guiding beliefs, organizational culture, approaches to conflict, and relationships to power.

Chapter 5, *Levers of Change*, considers what makes real and sustained change possible, including pacing and ways of helping people move into and live in new possibilities.

Chapter 6, *Transformational Change is Hard Work*, explores how consultants can manage key barriers to change. It includes the critical importance of confronting and not skirting around the pernicious forces of racism and systemic oppression and addressing the inevitability of resistance.

Chapter 7, *Creating Meaningful Meetings*, explores the logistical and spiritual aspects of meetings, which are where I spend the bulk of my time as a consultant. It describes how to design and conduct meetings and processes to create understanding, alignment, and clarity while supporting equity and inclusion.

Chapter 8, *Facilitating: Holding Space*, considers what it means to be a facilitator who holds tender processes for others. It covers skills and stances related to listening and asking questions, synthesizing conversations, and showing up "in the room" as our most fully authentic selves in the service of others.

# 1

# What Is a Transformational Consultant?

*Transformation requires us to actively seek to liberate ourselves from the thinking that surrounds us, from the habits of action we have internalized, both as individuals and in groups.*

— Miki Kashtan

I frequently get requests to meet with people who are considering going into consulting. Whenever possible, I find time to speak with them. People were very generous with me when I was starting out, and I want to be a part of building a consulting ecosystem for justice that is grounded in generosity and sharing knowledge.

Each conversation is slightly different, as each person's needs, interests, and experiences are unique. Sometimes their questions are largely logistical: How do I find clients? How do I bill? How much money should I charge? Sometimes they are more soul-searching: How do I know what my consulting offer is? What is the best way for me to contribute to the world?

A few years ago, I had the pleasure of speaking with Wren, a talented young person who had requested an informational interview. "I want to do what you do," they explained, "but I don't want to call myself a consultant. Maybe I could call it something else?"

I understand where this sentiment comes from; consultants are often seen as opportunistic people who charge a lot of money to deliver vague and useless products. There is no regulation or licensing for consulting, no industry standards we are expected to meet. And there is a lot of dubious behavior. An old joke goes "consultants take your watch and tell you the time."

This is the opposite of how I view myself and my work. I am proud of what I do, and I am proud to call myself an organizational development consultant. I define organizational development as processes that help organizations become more effective. I see my work as creating contexts within which people — myself and others — can rise to our highest and best selves and together do meaningful work that contributes to the world.

Synonyms for my role as a consultant might be: accompanier-who-helps-us-align-with-our-aspirations; guide-through-tricky-waters-who-brings-out-the-best-in-us; or trusted-person-who-sees-us-and-our-whole-system-with-compassion-tells-us-the-truth-and-helps-us-get-ourselves-to-a-better-place. A client once described me as a midwife for their movement, facilitating something new that wanted to be born. I love this!

For some people, the primary advantages of consulting include having control over your schedule and increased freedom and flexibility. These are great, but they are by no means my favorite things about consulting. For me, the best thing about consulting is enhancing the work of others who long for a more just and sustainable world and are committed to learning to follow that call as powerfully as possible.

Organizations bring me in at moments of change, conflict, and opportunity. Whether they are planning to clarify and build for the future, looking for leadership or team development, seeking news ways to operate outside of oppression, or simply trying to make their work more effective and impactful, my clients are in a space of vulnerability and need. I have the honor of coming in from the outside and lifting up their desire to transform into something better. This brings out the best in me and creates a space for them to enter a place of curiosity and learning to bring about the change they seek.

In this chapter, we'll explore transformational consulting, how it differs from other types of consulting and internal leadership, and what it can look like.

## Types of Consulting

Edgar Schein distinguished between three consulting postures:

- Expert: You are brought in to find solutions based on your content expertise.
- Pair of Hands: You are hired to do a task that a staff member could do, but the organization doesn't have the staff capacity.
- Collaborative: You are brought in to join the client on a journey of discovery and transformation.

From the beginning, my work has fit mainly in the third category. Schein calls consulting for transformational change "process consulting." I use the term transformational consulting, which I first learned from Robert Gass and the Social Transformation Project. Transformational consultants guide clients to arrive at new perspectives, stretch to new thinking, and discover new visions of what's possible and new ways of operating.

Transformational consulting differs significantly from "expert" consulting. Experts use their content expertise to identify solutions and present them to the client for implementation. Expert consultation is important when organizations need technical understanding for something they don't know how to do or figure out.

I am a process expert. I know how to co-create and facilitate processes that support people to arrive at and embrace the solutions that will work best for them. I've found that most people, regardless of what they say or think they want, will not be invested in the success of something they are simply told to do. Lesley University's former Center for Peaceable Schools, a group I had the honor of being part of for many years, called this transformational approach "Working With, Not Doing To."

In acupuncture school, I learned that acupuncturists use our Qi (energy) when we insert needles to stimulate a patient's Qi to flow and restore balance. However, our Qi does not enter the patient's body. Instead, acupuncture stimulates the patient's own energy to heal. Similarly, transformational consultants use our presence and tools to facilitate a system's power and wisdom to stimulate its own healing and health.

My job is not to have the "right" answers for my clients. I often couldn't have them even if I wanted to! Rather, I facilitate processes for clients to co-create solutions, which involves a lot more listening than speaking. They have an intimate knowledge of their situation that I, as an outsider, will never have.

At the same time, I bring my own wisdom and perspective to my clients. I push them to test if their assumptions are sound. I pose alternative scenarios if they do not see the full range of possibility. I let them know if I think they are heading in a wrong direction and suggest ideas and interpretations for them to push against as they dig deeper. I hold them to see beyond what they currently see, challenge them to stretch into new awareness, information, and growth, and encourage them as they decisively move forward.

There are certainly advantages and payoffs to an "expert" consulting posture, and I sometimes find them seductive. Having an outsider direct solutions can move things along much faster. The appreciation and approbation for quick wins and the rush of "knowing" the answers and fixing problems can be ego boosts. But we need to recognize and resist these temptations; for organizations seeking to embody justice, solutions are most effective and sustainable when created by them and with them rather than for them.

My client, Peony Hills, had a successful 25-year history as a retreat center. But over the last several years, it had drifted from its mission and taken on several new and seemingly

4

unrelated programs. People involved in the organization had many differing (and sometimes competing) ideas about what they stood for and what they should be doing. The board was at odds about the direction in which they should head, so they formed a committee to clarify the organization's core beliefs and purpose.

The committee had seven members representing different facets of the organization, consisting of staff from various departments and levels, board members and one key customer. They also had a mandate to be thoughtful, take the time needed to consider the existential issues at hand, and produce a revised mission and clear organizational values. These would become the foundation for clarifying the organization's identity and direction. Everyone understood that the future of Peony Hills rested on this effort.

I was engaged to facilitate the committee's ongoing work. They agreed to meet virtually, as often as needed, for several months until they were done. We met in a series of two-hour sessions over Zoom. Some committee members didn't know each other well when we began. To build trust across their many lines of difference, including race, age, sexual orientation, and history and position within the organization, we spent the first two sessions sharing personal stories and building relationships.

I invited the group into a practice of deep listening as they spoke about their personal histories and identities and why the organization was important to them. They developed meaningful connections with each other over the course of several meetings and were able to have increasingly heartfelt and sometimes difficult conversations. With respect, patient listening, and courageous truth-telling, they challenged their own and each other's beliefs and assumptions about what the organization stood for. This enabled them to create common ground about who Peony Hills was, what they believed in, and what they were here to do.

When they had a hard time articulating this consensus, I wrote a version of their values based on what I had heard them say. What I wrote didn't quite work for them, but it sparked their creative resolve. Committee members took the essence of my version and restated it in their own powerful words. The final product was beautiful and uniquely theirs.

I had the honor of guiding and accompanying them, speaking the truth of what I saw, pushing them when they were stuck, and holding space for them to tenderly navigate through challenging terrain. But the transformative power and clarity of their new mission and values came from them.

It can be hard for some folks to eschew the benefits of being an "expert" and knowing the answers. Many of us who were conditioned into paradigms of dominance need to rewrite our notions of what smart and valuable look like. From my experience, this gets much easier with practice, where I have been buoyed by the results of accompanying people as they discover their own wisdom and power.

## Consulting Offers

*Don't ask what the world needs. Ask what makes you come alive and go do it. Because what the world needs is people who have come alive.*

— Howard Thurman

Consulting offers are the services we can provide clients as they seek to build organizational effectiveness. There is a beautiful concept in Japanese, "Ikigai": the intersection of what the world needs, what you're good at, what you love to do, and what you can be paid for. Our ideal offers lie in this sweet spot.

Organizational development consultants have many possible offers. These include:

- Retreat and meeting facilitation
- Planning (strategic and otherwise)
- Leadership development
- Coaching
- Conflict resolution
- Team development
- Processes to advance racial justice
- Fund development
- Evaluation
- Organizational re-design

Some consultants have many offers, even mixing organizational development with other fields of expertise to open up a larger pool of potential work. But having too many offers also has downsides. First, it can be confusing for potential clients to wade through everything we say we can do in order to figure out if we can do what they need. Second, it can inhibit us from growing specific skill, as in the case of "Jack of all trades, master of none." When folks are starting out, though, it can be helpful to experiment with different offers to learn more about what we're good at and what we enjoy doing.

I started with a much longer list of offers than I currently have. I refined the list over the years as I got clearer about what I enjoy doing and the types of engagements that energize me. For instance, early in my consulting career, I offered conflict resolution and leadership coaching as stand-alone services.

I have training and experience in these areas, so I sometimes entered engagements specifically to facilitate conflicts or coach leaders. Though this was good and important work, over time I learned that I find these activities the most rich and rewarding when I do them in service of an overall organizational development initiative. My curiosity and presence go deeper and my wisdom shows up with greater clarity and power when I am more invested in the larger context of the system as a whole.

I still facilitate plenty of conflict resolution and leadership coaching, but only with people I am already working with in service of systemic change. Systems change requires individual transformation. While it is inspiring to witness sacred moments of individual and relationship growth, they are most meaningful and powerful for me when I see them as part of ongoing systems transformation. Fortunately, I have skilled and talented colleagues I can point clients toward when they are only looking for these specific services.

I have also added to my consulting offers. Most significantly, as I have grown in my understanding and analysis of racial injustice and systemic oppression, deepened my awareness of my own identity and social location as a white consultant, and built cherished partnerships with consultants who are Black, Indigenous, and other people of color, organizational development for racial justice has become an important aspect of my work.

My advice is this: don't be afraid to try new things or to let go of offers that no longer interest you. When you show up from a place of excitement, inspiration, and genuine curiosity, you are bringing your best self to your clients and yourself.

## Consulting Rhythms

I sometimes think about maintaining a consulting practice as like cooking a big feast on a grill. Things cook at different speeds and times. Each item has its specific preparation and cooking process. Everything needs tending, but some food requires more attention, some needs more time, the grill has a finite cooking space, and we want every dish to be delicious.

At any point in my consulting practice, I might be working on a handful of multi-month or even year-long planning processes, a few multi-year change processes, and regular retreats, check-ins, or smaller projects with clients I've had for many years. Each of these projects needs different amounts and kinds of time and tending.

As an independent consultant, I manage all the aspects of my own projects. Many consultancies are organizations in and of themselves; some small with only a few consultants and some enormous with thousands. They have managers, teams, associates, support staff, and partners. While this model has many benefits, most notably a deep bench of service providers and built-in collegiality, mutual learning, and support, I choose to be an independent consultant and work for myself, often partnering with other independent consultants. My independence allows me the flexibility to work with clients who are the best fit for me and to schedule at a pace and rhythm that best matches my energy, as well as the ability to flexibly adjust my fee when it is needed.

Independent consulting is not for the faint of heart. This is not because the work itself is hard, though it can be, but because the context within which it happens is so outside of typical work rhythms. It is almost an alternative universe where all the dimensions of time, space, and money differ from the norms of US culture. Here's what I mean:

- **Erratic schedule:** My calendar is never consistent from week to week. This is exciting on the one hand — I love the diverse ways I use my time and the shifting rhythms.

    With enough notice, I can usually block off time for myself when I want to — for an event I want to attend, a long weekend visit with friends, or to help a friend or family member with a medical appointment. This freedom is incredible. At the same time, I may have free time in the middle of a weekday while working weekends and evenings to facilitate retreats for clients or meet deadlines. I have learned to make good use of unscheduled time and not regret beautiful weekend days spent in airports and retreat centers.

- **Unpredictable workload:** It is an art, more than a science, to know how much work to take. My ideal workload is a delicate balance. I seek to be well-occupied and meaningfully engaged but never so busy that I can't tend to unforeseen client needs and my own well-being. There is a zone of enough but not too much that works for me. This may sound vague, but I don't think there's a formula that is the same for everyone across the board. I have a range of annual income that can meet my needs and an ideal range of time I want to work each week. This has varied over the years as my kids have grown, family members and I have faced health complications, and other commitments have required my time and attention. I have mostly been able to stay inside this zone, which sometimes means turning down work I would very much like to do and learning not to panic if it's looking like I might take a dip into not quite enough.

- **Irregular income:** Most employment comes with a regular paycheck. Not so independent consulting. I do not have benefits, paid time off, paid health insurance, or a company retirement plan. I need to think of my income in much larger blocks of time — months and even by year — and I need to make sure my hourly and daily rates cover the benefits that a regular job would provide: health insurance, disability insurance, vacation, sick time, etc. The absence of a steady and dependable paycheck can be a limiting barrier to the field for people who don't have the privilege of some fallback or cushion as they begin consulting.

When I started consulting, my schedule was much more variable, an unpredictable roller coaster of feast or famine. It took a couple of years and all the patience I could muster as I got clearer on my offers, cultivated my network, and built up to a consistently full practice.

## Consultant Postures

In his brilliant, complicated, infuriating, and life-changing book *The 7 Habits of Highly Effective People*, Steven Covey details three stances that can be applied to work:

- Control: We have a lot of capacity to impact outcomes.
- Influence: We do not have direct control but can impact outcomes through persuasion, encouragement, inspiration, and guidance.
- Concern: We care about something but have no tangible ability to impact outcomes.

Our power as transformational consultants lies squarely in our ability to influence. We do not have the power to make things happen, like an executive director or internal organizational leader, but the personal power and clarity we bring to our clients is a force not to be underestimated. I must be at once wholly committed to helping my clients reach the intended outcomes of our engagement and unattached to any outcomes beyond that. Once the engagement has ended, the fruits of our work are completely out of my hands, which can be really hard because I care a great deal about my clients and their work.

The consulting stance can confer wisdom and "authority," though the lenses through which our clients perceive our identities can filter how they receive us as consultants. As a small white woman, I have noticed that as I have aged and come to sport a head of powerful gray hair, clients often receive my wisdom with more gravity than they did when I was visibly younger. Still, our perceived authority is its own kind of power, and I need to be mindful of how I use it.

I cannot casually bandy about my power. Clients often take what I say very seriously, so I must be intentional with my words as well my actions. I must be mindful of meeting the pull toward any kind of "power over" or dominance from a place of wisdom and curiosity. My job is to lift everybody up, not seat myself on top.

Consultants and their clients live in a unique orbit. My mentor and friend, Anne Litwin, introduced me to the very helpful frame of Affinity and Autonomy. To understand and earn people's trust in systems where I consult, I must relate, be relate-able and demonstrate through my actions that I really care about them: Affinity. At the same time, I must maintain sufficient distance to see the fuller picture of what is going on and not get fully sucked into the gravity of their condition: Autonomy.

My clients tend to be amazing human beings and the pull for affinity can be intense. I can find myself enamored of their brilliance and compassion, which can obscure my clarity of vision. My ability to see the bigger picture of their situation, help them see truths and possibilities that are not yet visible to them, and offer tools to help them build new pathways is what makes me useful. I must be mindful of maintaining my independence of thought outside their system to provide the external perspective and care that are among the primary values of a consultant.

I continually check in with myself to ensure that I breathe metaphorical fresh air from outside the systems I'm working in. I need to see the stories inside the organization without the full force of the gravitational pull they have on the inside.

I see my engagement as an opportunity to lift everyone up and help the organizational culture shine to its best. But I must keep affinity and autonomy in mind. I can't let my client's fondness for me, or mine for them, get in the way of telling the truth and interrupting harmful or dysfunctional systems or behaviors.

## Rooting in Ourselves

*I feel there is a big contradiction. There are seven billion human beings and nobody wants to have problems or suffering, but there are many problems and much suffering, most of our own creation. Why? Something is lacking. As one of the seven billion human beings, I believe everyone has a responsibility to develop a happier world. We need, ultimately, to have a greater concern for others' well-being. In other words, kindness or compassion, which is lacking now. We must pay more attention to our inner values. We must look inside.*

— The 14th Dalai Lama

I used to think that Peter Block's *Flawless Consulting*, considered by many to be an essential guide for consultants, had a tongue-in-cheek title. "Flawless is impossible!" I thought. I interpret the title differently now. We all make many mistakes, and I am always learning to do things differently and better. I believe Block is saying that "Flawless" means rigorously striving to act with integrity, to show up as fully and as honestly as we can, to hold our clients with dignity, and to learn from our mistakes.

I often think of a comment made by an interviewee in Otto Scharmer's book *Theory U*: "The quality of an intervention depends entirely on the internal condition of the intervener." Quantum mechanics shows that there is no such thing as a neutral observer. Our presence impacts and changes every situation just because we are there. I do not see the system as it was before I arrived. I see it as it is, influenced by me, for the energy I bring impacts every situation I am in.

I worried a lot about this when I started consulting. I am certainly not always in a state of gratitude and presence; nobody is. My wounds, learned dominance, fears, and quirks all dwell within me. If my energy and state of being are constantly impacting what is happening, how can I dare to show up in my fully flawed self, warts and all?

As Lama Rod Owens has said, "I cannot help to resource others if I am under resourced while trying to help others. I end up draining resources from others without their consent."

Over the years, I've learned that personal healing is essential if we want to show up as clearly and fully as possible and to have grace with ourselves when we don't. My commitment to behaving with integrity, acting in alignment with my values, staying faithful in my words, and delivering the highest quality consulting I can requires me to attend continually to my inner growth and well-being.

Practices that regulate my nervous system and help me understand my inner workings enable me to hold my own humanity and fallibility truthfully and, often, compassionately. Yoga, meditation, lots of time among plants and trees, gardening, hiking, and walking along the river near my home; time with beloved humans and pets, colleagues, family, and friends; and Jewish spiritual practices such as Mussar (the study of Jewish ethics) all help me to resource my internal self and have shifted how I move in my body and the world.

It takes a lot of practice to learn the rhythms of consulting, move humbly with our clients, and continually root into ourselves. My advice for newer consultants, and for myself, is to go slowly, be patient with ourselves, be present, and always tend to our inner resources as we seek to hold space for others.

## My Experience as a White Consultant

Over years of learning, particularly through the generosity of Black, Indigenous, and other people of color sharing their lived experience with me personally and through trainings and media, I have come to understand that racism is deeply embedded within me, as it is within all institutions and people in the US and perhaps on earth. The cost to me of complicity with this force — which outwardly benefits me as it harms others — is no less than the fullness of my humanity. Unlearning racism is a reclamation of humanity, both for people targeted by its brutal impact and for those of us socialized to perpetuate its cruelty. It is spiritual healing for me as I develop a deeper relationship with myself, my body, and my place as a human on this earth.

More than 25 years ago, I sat surrounded by shelves piled high with books in the living room of my then professor, the late Steven Brion-Meisels. His pet bird squawked gently in the background. It was the week before I would graduate with a master's degree, and I wanted to think with him, a white man dedicated to racial justice, about my role as a white person.

"I just don't think I'm worthy of doing this work," I said, uncomfortably aware of how far I had to go in unlearning white supremacy inside myself. How could I, so steeped in my social conditioning, authentically contribute to the healing that is so desperately needed to create a more just world? I worried about all the unintentional harm I might do and had already done. "I don't think of it that way," he replied. "It's not about worthy or noble. It's the work that needs to be done. It's messy and hard, and white people need to be a part of it." In his kind and compassionate way, Steven's clear message was, "Don't let your privilege and your comfort hold you back from doing what needs to be done."

And still, for the first several years I consulted, I told myself I didn't know enough, I would surely fuck up, and I really, really didn't want to cause harm. I saw my role as lifting up issues around racism and racial justice within organizations and with white people who did not yet understand the impact of racism in their work. It was often the first time the truth of racism was spoken aloud in these predominantly white organizations. I imagined myself opening a door and demonstrating that white people cannot look away from the dehumanizing cruelty of the system of racialization.

But when my clients were ready to go through the door and commit to addressing racism, I referred them to consultants who were Black, Indigenous, or other people of color. I worried that I might appropriate and misrepresent others' experiences or take on work that was not my place to do.

This was my stance for many years until I finally came to see that I was making choices to maintain my comfort and not have to figure out new ways of being. Patient, loving colleagues and friends and deepening spiritual practices helped me learn to let go of some of the white shame that had previously gripped me along with my fear of "getting it wrong." I saw how critically important it is for white people, for me, to be fully accountable for undoing racism in partnership with Black, Indigenous, and other people of color. Laying the entire burden of the work on Black and Brown consultants can force additional, and sometimes traumatic, labor.

My commitment to eradicating racism and systems of oppression means continually coming into deeper relationship with the complexities of how I occupy my identity, particularly my whiteness. It means continually building my understanding of the historical factors that got us here and their current impact. It means speaking the truth about what I know and don't know with care and being willing to listen and own when I make mistakes. It means attending carefully to when my voice is a contribution and when I need to stand aside. It means constantly checking in with myself about what is true and knowing I can never fully understand the full truth that is other people's experience. It means speaking up and standing up when racism is present.

This commitment also requires me to continually examine and contradict my dominant impulses — to move forward too quickly or to imagine I know something I do not yet know. Although many years of practice have given me greater comfort and ease with not believing or following these impulses, I understand that this will be a lifelong challenge.

A colleague once asked how I knew I was ready to engage more deeply and proactively in organizational development racial justice work. There is no certification that lets white people know when we have reached a point where we can trust ourselves to do more good than harm, to attend to the harm we do, and to learn to do better. People of all racialized identities begin doing this work when they are not yet ready, which for many white people is often when we do not yet understand the history and contours of structural racism and how whiteness and supremacy have impacted and continue to live within us.

My own turning point was when Black colleagues and other colleagues of color whom I trusted started looking to partner with me on organizational development racial justice projects. I understood this as an affirmation and have embraced these partnerships. As a white person, I will still inevitably miss and misunderstand the experiences and needs of people who are Black, Indigenous, and other people of color as well as the devious ways that racism and dominance infect systems, leaders, and myself. But the things that I may miss are critical for the success of the interventions we are facilitating, which is one reason these partnerships are so important.

Trying to find my footing as a white racial justice consultant has been a painful lesson in unlearning perfectionism. Although I know there is no way to get it perfectly right, I am still wrestling with my longing for perfection even as I write this. I need to let go of my white saviorism while not letting my colleagues who are Black, Indigenous, and other people of color carry the emotional burden of the racism present in our engagements. I need to follow the leadership of consultants who are Black, Indigenous, and other people of color while also taking responsibility for my own choices and presence. I need to fully own my power in cross-race partnerships while showing up in my whiteness in a way that allows my colleagues to shine fully. I need to step into places where I might be tempted to let my partners handle something alone, particularly if it involves conflict and emotion, while not dominating.

Among other incredible colleagues, I am blessed to partner with Melinda Barbosa. There are multiple dimensions of difference between us. Melinda is a Black woman who is over 20 years younger than me and introduces herself as the youngest of 50 first cousins. I am white and the oldest child in my family of origin. When we undertook a joint inquiry about our work together, Melinda suggested a framing question: "What is true about how we move together?" Here are a few of the things we noticed:

- We talk explicitly about power and how our identities impact our partnership. We are blessed with clients who are with us on the journey of undoing racism, and we are transparent with them about the choices we make regarding our roles, processes, and thinking.
- We share a commitment to asking when we don't understand something. We are honest and vulnerable about what we may not know and do not judge each other. For me, this often means checking in and asking for feedback if I am unsure about how I am occupying space.
- We check in as often as we need to before, during, and after a session with a client. When something needs attention

or intervention during a session, we check which of us should address it. Sometimes this happens in the blink of an eye: with a glance, we know who will step in.

- Melinda noted that it is helpful for her when I see and name white people's dominant behaviors as the result of shame and fear, as she can see and experience those behaviors as oppressive. I can tend to the person, compassionately redirect, and help them notice the impact of their behavior with dignity. This lifts emotional labor from her.

- We talk openly with each other and with our clients about our fees and how we honor both my years of experience and the emotional and psychic burden that working with a white colleague in predominantly white organizations places on consultants who are Black, Indigenous, and other people of color. In contracting with our clients, we are clear about the extra time we need to process what comes up and continue to learn from each other, and that Melinda may need for recovery.

- We are committed to remaining in human connection with each other. As Melinda said, "it's messy." There is no one correct answer or perfect way to be.

Over dinner at a retreat Melinda and I co-facilitated for a multiracial staff, one of the participants asked us to talk about how we navigate our partnership. We spoke honestly and vulnerably about the centrality of telling each other our truth. I believe that the trust visible in our partnership across our multiple differences and the ways we transparently navigate and communicate offer our clients a model for holding and sharing power across many dimensions of difference.

# 2

# The Business of Practice

*To live outside the law, you must be honest.*

— Bob Dylan

Early in my career as an acupuncturist, in the days before some insurances covered treatment, I noticed an insidious tension. The more unwell my clients were, the more care they needed. In the classic fee-for-service model, I earned more money caring for people who were not well, many of whom were suffering economic hardship because of their illnesses or had few economic resources to begin with.

There is a similarly rooted contradiction in consulting. My purpose is to bring about transformation toward justice, love, equity, and care while operating inside of the ultimate transactional context: our racialized capitalist economy. I exchange my time, energy, skill, care, and wisdom for money to sustain and benefit me and my family; that exchange often takes place with organizations who have limited resources.

I seek to practice with integrity inside of this pernicious paradox. I try to strike a balance between honoring my livelihood and not allowing it in any way to drive my services or relationships with my clients.

This chapter explores how I have constructed an independent consulting practice that seeks to model "being the change" while living in the impossible contradictions of racialized capitalism. It wrestles with fundamental questions about transformational consulting as a business. How do we build our practice, determine our scope of service, and set fees? How do we set clear agreements and hold ourselves and our clients accountable? How do we conduct our practices to prefigure and call forth the world we want while supporting our own economic needs?

## Building a Practice

"Well, not marketing, but more thinking about how I put myself out there," said a colleague one day as he was pondering how to build his practice.

Marketing is a dirty word in some circles. It conjures up images of Mad Men skillfully selling people goods they don't need and corporations manufacturing desire out of false scarcity; inauthentic at best, devious and evil at its too frequent worst. But when we take away nefarious intent, we can look at marketing simply as sharing what we have to offer so that the people who want to work with us can.

People sometimes ask me how I find clients. I prefer to ask how I help the right clients find me.

Consultants market themselves by presenting at conferences, sending out regular online newsletters, keeping a strong presence on listservs, posting on social media, publishing, blogging, podcasting, and building good websites. These strategies may work well for you, and you should definitely use them if they do.

But following Robert Gass, who says we should "be" our offer, I think about marketing through the lens of authentic human connection. While I have a website — and labor intensively every time I update it — I have found it useful only as a place for people who meet or hear about me to find out more. I have never (not EVER in all these years) gotten a new client because they landed on my website cold and decided to hire me.

My key marketing strategy is to connect and stay connected with people I like. My hope is that authentic connection, shared curiosity, genuine interest, and trust will enliven and mutually enrich each of us and our work. Knowing what other people are up to inspires me, builds my sense of solidarity and companionship, and expands my imagination of what could be possible — and I hope it does the same for them. If I think of myself as my brand, this strategy aligns deeply with my values and the way I approach my work and life.

When I was first building my consulting practice, I committed to doing ten networking activities each week and over the years I've kept up the practice. I have pretty strong extroverted tendencies, so this has typically been energizing for me, though it may not work as well for folks who are not energized by connecting with others. My definition of networking includes:

- Going to events, talks, and workshops put on by people who interest me.
- Taking walks with people.
- Sending a "hello" email to someone who is on my mind.
- Obliging, if I can, when asked for a favor or advice.
- Meeting someone for a cup of tea or lunch, in person or on Zoom.
- Running into someone unexpectedly and having a good connection, even if it's brief.
- Going to a meeting or event and making a real connection with someone.
- Sending an article or podcast to someone I think will also value it.

Ten networking activities (or points of contact) a week may sound daunting, but it's not hard for me to achieve. This early commitment ensured that I continued building my network of authentic relationships even if I was over-the-top busy or not feeling much like connecting. Over time, sharing connection and learning became an unconscious part of my life, part of my muscle memory. These days, I rarely think about reaching a quota, but when I look back on a week, I generally see that I've made at least ten connections just in the course of doing what I do.

How is this a marketing strategy? Although my goal is always to share connection and learning, not to find work, I trust that people in my network will spread the word about me and my skills, just as I spread information about folks I see doing good work. This has borne fruit. Almost all my engagements come from satisfied clients and people in my networks passing my name along, sometimes many years later. The bonus is that most of the people referred to me are doing things I want to support in ways that match my values and commitments.

My take-home marketing message is an invitation to do what is authentic for you, whether you are just starting out or have been in practice for a while. For me, that's connection. Whatever makes you feel good about representing yourself is the right branding and marketing strategy for you.

## Colleagues and Collaborators

I once saw an excellent documentary called *The Journey*. It was a low-budget, independent film about a recent college graduate's search for wisdom and meaning as he transitioned to his newly-minted adult life. He traveled by van around the US, asking "successful" people for advice. One gem he heard has stayed with me: "Somebody's ability to be successful is directly proportional to their ability to ask for help."

Although I am an independent consultant, I could not sustain my work without trusted colleagues. I have grown so much as a consultant and as a human being from the gift of my collegial relationships. For me, this kind of growth and collaboration happens within three structures:

1. **Collegial relationships:** I have quite a few colleagues who are also consultants. I meet with many folks once or several times a year for lunch, tea, calls, or walks. I treasure these relationships, some of which have blossomed into friendships, although others have stayed in the professional realm.

We share information about what we are learning, what we are seeing, what's challenging, and what's joyful. I am happy to be a "phone-a-friend" for many of them and have been blessed by their generous listening ears when I have needed company thinking through thorny challenges. Many of these folks are also part of my referral pool. Since I cannot accommodate all the requests I receive, I am happy to be able to refer to skilled colleagues.

2. **Consultants group:** I am part of a group of consultants that has been meeting monthly for over 15 years. We think together about our roles and actions and give each other deep listening ears and honest feedback. I can't imagine consulting without this space to reflect, challenge my thinking, and deepen my practice.

3. **Partnerships:** I am very blessed to have several colleagues I partner with regularly. These are people with whom I have developed a special trust and alchemy over time. I have learned a lot from each of them, and I know that we can depend fully on each other when we work together. I am also blessed with a life partner, my husband Jonathan Rosenthal, whose work intersects with mine and who is a constant thinking partner.

When a client's budget and need allows, I try to partner with a colleague, though it is not always possible. I see immense value in facilitating with a trusted colleague, especially in low-trust systems and particularly across race. I imagine our trust as a kind of magnetic pull that can lift trust within the system. Modeling trust calls people to lean into the possibility of opening their hearts to a different way of being together. It can be difficult to stay grounded when I am holding space alone in situations of very low trust. Working with a partner grounds the work and helps us all stay connected to love and compassion.

I'm sure there are other ways for an independent practitioner to structure collaboration. Whatever model you choose, I cannot imagine doing this work to its fullest potential without my colleagues.

## Selecting Clients

"Your colleague/client/cousin/friend told us to call you. We really, really need your help. We need a new strategic plan/a retreat/any help you can give us. When can you start?" I've received countless versions of this call or email over the years. Even when I'm not as busy as I want to be, I've learned that it's never a good idea to just say yes. Conversely, even if I'm over-the-top busy, it's not a good idea to just say no.

The most important thing about taking on new clients is not how much work I need or have but whether we are a good fit for each other. I have found that the more aligned I am with my client's values, the better the outcomes of our engagement and the more satisfied I am. Sometimes this means saying no to a gig that looks great on paper, sometimes it means asking a client if they are willing to wait. Sometimes I regret having to pass up opportunities, but when the stars align, I am able to take on the right clients at the right time.

Unlike consultants who specialize in particular issue areas (e.g., environmental justice), I choose my clients because they are challenging the status quo of dominance, dehumanization, and extraction. I am committed to working with people and organizations advancing racial, environmental, social, gender, and economic justice. In practice, my clients are often small and midsized non-profits or local governments with an explicit social justice mission (e.g., restorative justice, ending domestic violence, transforming food and agricultural systems). They can also be social enterprises (e.g., fair trade companies) and even local governments and services committed to equity (e.g., libraries, schools, human services, transportation).

I see strong distinctions between consulting to formal organizations, decentralized movements, and coalitions. Within these different types of systems, people have different kinds and levels of accountability to each other and their shared work. I prefer to work in organizations and coalitions that have structural as well as interpersonal and ideological accountability. Those kinds of boundaries make the most sense to me. Decentralized movements operate in more open or dynamic ways, often driven primarily by accountability to ideals and values.

It does help to know enough about my clients' content areas to be comfortable with their language and the critical issues they face. Some process consultants don't consider this important, but I want to be sufficiently versed to know whether they are talking about important issues or pursuing distractions that won't serve them.

When considering a new client, I usually research the organization, then schedule an initial call to learn more. In that first conversation, I ask the following questions:

- What are you looking to do?
- Why now? What is the current condition or question that brings you to this work?
- Why is doing this work important to your organization? To you?
- If our work together is successful, where do you hope to be and what do you hope to know at the end?
- What ideas or needs do you have about how the work will get done? (e.g., a deadline or something that needs to be completed before this work begins).
- What challenges are we likely to encounter?
- What resources do you have for doing this work? (e.g., financial resources, staff time, support services).
- What do you know about what you need to do? What do you not know?

- What are you looking for in a consultant? What will make an engagement successful from your perspective?

These questions, the follow up questions they naturally generate, the tone of the conversation, and the feeling I get from it help me know enough about the client to discern if we are a good fit for each other.

My ideal clients share my commitment to a just and sustainable world and are willing to continually learn, look within themselves, and tell the truth about themselves and the world as they see it. Here are some criteria I use to determine if a potential client is a good fit for me:

- *What work are they looking to do?*
  - Is it interesting to me?
  - Does it align with what I can and want to do?
  - Can I learn something from this engagement that I am curious about?
- *Are our styles a good fit?*
  - Do their values and vision align with mine?
  - Do they resonate with my approach?
  - Do I resonate with the way they operate?
  - Do I feel good when I connect with the people?
  - Will I enjoy working with them?
- *Are they ready to do the work?*
  - Is what they are asking for the right step at this time?
  - Do they have the leadership to champion the project and follow through?
  - Do they have the will and support to do the work?
  - Do they want to look at themselves, learn, and operate differently?
  - Are they willing to stretch themselves, both personally and organizationally, as they learn more about themselves and their world?

- ○ Will they give the work the time, resources, and care it needs to succeed?
- *Am I the right fit?*
  - ○ Do I have what they are looking to do in my skill set? If not, is it possible that I could bring in someone else with this skill set or easily build the skills myself?
  - ○ Will my identity be a fit for this group? If my identity would pose challenges, I look to partner with or refer to another consultant.
  - ○ Am I geographically well situated for the work? I have had several queries from potential clients in other parts of the US where there are many good consultants. If it is a long-term piece of work, having a local consultant may make more environmental, financial, and logistical sense for them.

While all these factors are important to me and my ideal clients evoke a "Yes!" in all categories, I sometimes need to take engagements that don't meet all my criteria. The tension between being discerning about clients and needing to earn money can impact a consultant's choices, particularly when starting a practice. I have also loosened my criteria when I have room in my schedule or a client is particularly compelling. But no matter how alluring or economically prudent these choices may be, I always end up regretting taking on clients who are not a good fit or are not ready to do the work they need to do.

Some consultants feel they need to say yes to everything that comes along for economic reasons, regardless of fit. I hear this concern and it's valid, but over the long term I don't believe it effectively builds and sustains a practice. When the fit is not good, the quality of the engagement is never as good as I would like it to be. When we take on engagements that exhaust us and don't result in good work, our brand suffers and less work can come our way. We may think we can't afford to say no, but also we often can't afford the vicious cycle that results when we don't say no.

If I don't think a prospective client is a fit, I refer them to someone in my network who I think will better serve them. My decision about fit usually boils down to one (or more) of the following issues:

- I don't have time to do what they want on their timeline.
- My identity as a straight, cis-gendered, older, white woman will not serve them if I work alone (rather than as part of a multi-racial consulting team).
- The work they are doing is not within my area of expertise and/or is not aligned with my values.
- They do not seem truly curious to learn new things or approaches and would be better served by a transactional or expert consultant.

How do you know what's a good fit for you? Clarifying your values and criteria goes a long way, but we can't always know for sure. Sometimes we need to stretch and see what we find.

Bill was a board member of The Good Lights Project (GLP), a non-profit renewable energy education and advocacy group. I had worked with GLP for several years on strategic planning, leadership development, conflict resolution, and executive transition. I loved working with them. The board and staff were fun, engaged, and committed. Bill was a great board member: kind, generous, smart, and hardworking. He was funny and compassionate, and I really enjoyed working with him.

When Bill asked me to consult with his company, I was excited. I told him I had never worked with a for-profit company without a social mission before and I knew little about his sector, building supply distribution. But he was confident that I was the right fit to do some planning and team development for his company, so I said yes.

Two months later, the 12 members of Bill's senior staff and I came together for a retreat. I had worked with a smaller planning team from the group, including conducting 1:1 assessment interviews with each member of the planning team to set the purpose, outcomes and process for the retreat. I knew them to be kind and thoughtful people. Yet, when I drove in past the massive golf course at the swanky resort in Florida where we were meeting, entered the marble-covered lobby, and saw that the guests were entirely white and the only Black, Indigenous, and other people of color were staff, my spirit sank.

"What the hell am I doing here, and how did I let this happen?" I asked myself as shame and regret washed over me.

I took a deep breath and committed to showing up as fully as possible. I was here to do work, and I was here to help Bill.

We were highly successful according to the conventional markers. People enjoyed the retreat, and we achieved our original purpose and desired outcomes. If you watched a video, you would say everything went well. But there was no way around the fact that maximizing profits was the core of their work. Many conversations revolved around the compromises and strategies they were willing to make to do that — environmental and social compromises that were way beyond my comfort zone. I pointed them out when I heard them emerging, as Bill had asked me to do, but most went forward anyway.

Afterwards, I had the sick feeling of betraying myself and my values. I had performed well, and Bill was delighted with our work. But I was exhausted, depleted, and disappointed with myself for a long time afterward. The engagement had been a stretch for me, one I undertook willingly but ended up regretting. I learned a valuable lesson and have not worked again with an organization that has such different values from mine, no matter how much I might like the people involved.

I believe that the sustainability of my consulting practice rests on working in alignment with my values and integrity. Alignment comes in different forms. I have challenged my assumptions and boundaries around who at first glance I think that I can work with, often to a delightfully surprising result. You might find your alignment in totally different ways than I do. But regardless of how we find it, when we are in alignment with what we believe and what matters to us, our work enlivens us and fortifies our life energy, and we bring that energy to our clients.

## Contract with Care

*All summations have a beginning, all effect has a*
*story, all kindness begins with the sown seed.*

—Mary Oliver

Entering a consulting engagement is all about building relationship and trust between the consultant and client. Whether we are working with new or existing clients, we need to begin by articulating our contract with each other. The word "contract" may sound legalistic and cold when we're talking about building trusted relationships and working from a place of love, but I like the word and believe it is fundamental to consulting.

31

In *Flawless Consulting*, Peter Block asserts that the success of a consulting engagement is always dependent on having a good contract. I fully agree! A good contract gives us guard rails, helping us know what to expect of each other, how we will be in partnership, and how we will communicate around emerging or unmet expectations. The original contract then becomes the basis for ongoing conversations as we learn more about what is required for us to reach our shared goals. In other words, contracting is not a one-time event that initiates an engagement, Rather, it is a continual process of learning, aligning our expectations, and making sure that our structures and agreements continue to serve us.

One of the most important tools I use in my consulting engagements is the POP (Purpose, Outcomes and Process) framework developed by Leslie Sholl Jaffee and Randall Alford. It is foundational to everything that I do, starting with contracting (you will see POP referenced throughout this book and a more complete explanation can be found in the Tools and Resources at the end).

POP begins with clarity of Purpose, as everything flows from there. Once we know *why* we are doing something, we can identify the Outcomes we seek (the *what*) and lastly, the Processes we will use to get there (the *how*). Quite simply: POP. (See Tools and Resources.)

My contracting begins with what I call a contracting conversation. Clients often come to me with an idea of how our process should look. Sometimes they are spot on. Not infrequently, however, the process they have in mind lies somewhere on the continuum from wrong-thing-at-the-wrong-time to terribly misguided. This may stem from an unclear analysis of their current situation or an unclear understanding of process. I listen carefully to them and together we tease out their purpose and desired outcomes. Once these are clear, we can explore potential processes. I then put together a proposal based on our conversation.

It is not unusual to go through multiple rounds of discussion and proposals before we reach full agreement on the scope of our work. This is because the contracting process helps the client clarify what they are trying to do and how it will work best for them to do it. In other words, it is more the first chapter of the engagement than the prologue.

This raises the question of when to start charging for my work. The consulting firm Essential Partners taught me a rule of thumb: two conversations. Meet with the client twice. If the scope still isn't clear, contract to help them develop clarity about what kind of process they need (sometimes this entails me going inside the organization to learn more about it, which I discuss in the section about Discovery and Assessment in Chapter 3). I try my best to adhere to this rule, though it's not always possible.

A piece of advice I offer to newer consultants is: only contract as far as you can see. We don't want to bind ourselves to long-term contracts for the wrong scope of work. This might mean contracting only for an assessment that can reveal what the client actually needs, even when they offer a much bigger but vague contract from the start. You and your client must agree on the scope and expected results of your work.

Amid the enthusiasm and energy of the beginning of an engagement, it can be tempting to promise the moon in a contract with really high expectations. Years ago, I learned the idea of under-promising and over-delivering from my friend and client, Michael Rozyne. It has served me as a guide for many years. I don't run as fast as I can to overachieve. Instead, I only include in the contract what I know we can deliver well — and then we deliver those things with excellence, going further than called for where possible and appropriate.

I use the following outline to develop contracts, based on the POP framework:

1. The **Purpose:** Why the organization is doing this work at this time.
2. Our **Desired Outcomes:** What we will have accomplished at the end of our successful engagement.
3. The **Process** we will use and how we will do our work together, including:
   - **Tasks:** Articulating all the things that need to be done in order to reach our desired outcomes.
   - **Roles and Responsibilities:** How the consultant, the client, and other stakeholders will be part of the engagement: What specifically will I do? What will I not do? What will we do together? What can we depend on each other for?
   - **Timelines:** What will happen when? What kinds of agreements do we have about these timelines? Are they fixed? Where might there be flexibility?
   - **Payment:** How much I will be charging and the schedule and terms on which I will submit invoices for payment.
   - **Agreements between the client and myself:** How will we work together? What supports us each to do our best work? What are our expectations around communication and availability? What will we do if needs emerge that exceed the scope of this contract? What kinds of conversations will we have if we are moving faster or slower than we predicted? I also include a cancellation policy that articulates my expectations for payment if the client cancels within a certain timeframe.

I occasionally need to recontract in the middle of an engagement. Recontracting should happen anytime the scope or expectations shift. It is time to recontract if new or different outcomes emerge or if the process needs to be reconfigured to meet our stated outcomes. This can include allocating consulting time differently and may or may not change the fee or timeline.

Anytime anything shifts from our agreed-upon contract, I need to make sure my client and I have the same understanding about what is happening and why. This can involve a new written contract if the fee or outcomes shift significantly. A simple email can suffice if we are just adjusting a timeline or adding a task without changing the fee. This is an ounce of prevention against mismatched expectations down the line.

My colleague and I were hired as a multi-racial consulting team to facilitate a strategic planning process for Trees and the Sea, a relatively small but far-reaching organization committed to environmental, racial, and social justice.

Before we began, we learned from Lorraine, the white executive director, that there was a fair amount of tension among the multi-racial staff. The incongruence between what the organization valued (e.g., racial justice and healthy relationships) and how they were operating (e.g., with many unaddressed manifestations of white dominance culture such as urgency in all aspects of work) were causing misunderstanding, mistrust, and distress among the staff.

We knew from experience that if we moved forward with strategic planning without addressing the staff tension, the issues would either emerge in a heightened way during the planning process or go underground. Whichever path they took, they would ultimately undermine the efficacy of the plan and the health of the staff and organization. Fortunately, Lorraine was in alignment with our approach.

Agreeing to hold off on planning for a little while and attend to the staff tensions, we contracted to do an assessment to get a fuller picture of the current situation. We began by interviewing all the staff members. We learned there were significant hurts related to one incident that had vastly different impacts on Black, Indigenous and other staff of color, and white staff, as well as ongoing hurts from organizational habits of over work, which many understood to be symptoms of white organizational culture.

Once we better understood the issues, we developed a proposal for a facilitated process with the staff. My colleague and I met a few times with the full staff to frame the process, reflect back to them what we had learned through the assessment, and facilitate story sharing so they could better know one another and what had brought each of them to Trees and the Sea.

We also began meeting with them in ongoing racialized affinity spaces, me with the white staff and my colleague with the staff who were Black, Indigenous, and other people of color. These groups had different needs. The white group deepened their capacity to talk about race and racism and sit more fully in their impact, both within themselves and inside the organization. They built enough trust to help each other see where they were missing the impact of their dominant behaviors and listen to the feedback they were giving each other. The Black, Indigenous and people of color group built relationship and solidarity around recognizing, contradicting, and supporting each other not to collude with patterns of internalized oppression.

We had a series of mini-retreats with the whole staff and introduced skills and frameworks for dialogue, reframing conflict, and understanding how white dominance culture was playing out for everyone in the organization.

> We facilitated honest and meaningful conversations about their culture and the incident that had occurred. Over time, and with Lorraine's courageous leadership, the team built a culture of honest dialogue. We then agreed on a new contract for ongoing leadership and team development with the whole staff and anti-racism learning and un-learning in racialized affinity groups. When the organization was ready, we began strategic planning.

## Setting Fees

Money can bring a relationship into a transactional framework. I am committed to a different approach. While there is no one right way for consultants to handle fees and billing, it's important to me that my compensation feels fair to the client and to me. For me, a consulting contract is an opportunity for a fair exchange that supports the livelihoods of all involved, in this case the consultant (me!) and the client organization. I do not want my clients to see a cash register every time I walk in the door. I do want them to feel they have made a good investment. I want our engagement to nurture us both and our payment agreement to be a manifestation of that nurturing.

The irony of setting my fees is that I am looking to do work that moves us away from greed and materialism and I am doing that work within the context of capitalism. I typically exchange money for service, though sometimes in lieu of money I have traded my services for goods and services from board members or others.

In an informal 2021 poll, I found that non-profit consultants charge between $150 and $500 per hour, depending on their geographic market (e.g., rates are higher in New York City than in Boston) and the organization's size (e.g., larger non-profits and foundations pay at the higher end). Even in the lower range, these rates may sound high compared to the salaries in many non-profits. However, a consulting fee includes no benefits (e.g., health insurance, retirement, paid time off) or job security, so it shouldn't be considered on the same scale as a salary.

I have a regular rate that I offer most of my clients, and I have rarely had clients question it. If I really want to work with an organization that I sense (or know) may not be able to afford my regular rate, I tell them what it is and let them know I am willing to negotiate.

I determine my fee by starting with our desired outcomes and working backwards. If this is where we want to be, what are the tasks involved? Based on the tasks needed, my role, and the client's role, what exactly will I do? How long will that take? For some clients I propose a time range, for others a flat fee. It depends on the client's available resources, the scope of work, and how much clarity we have about process at the outset.

For a short engagement with a clear process (e.g., a one-off retreat), I tend to charge a flat fee. For longer engagements where it's impossible to tell how much time it will actually take, I propose a realistic range. It's also important to remember that the time I spend on official tasks is rarely the full measure of the value I bring to my clients. I've had significant breakthroughs in my thinking about our work in the shower, on walks, or while doing yoga, and I may need to spend time reading or consulting with a colleague to figure out how to address an issue.

For the first few years I consulted, I always charged a flat fee. Back then, I was often wildly off in my time estimates, and I didn't want my client (or myself) to worry about the cost once we had contracted. I only wanted us to get to a great result, no matter how much time it took on my part. While this could be frustrating financially (and some might call it ridiculous and naïve), I decided I was being paid to gain experience. However, I now believe that a range of time (and fee) is a better and fairer option for everyone.

As I have honed my skills, my time and fee estimates have become more accurate; an added bonus of experience!

Given the complex and contradictory notions of money in our capitalist society, there's no perfect way to set fees. But as you think about what you will charge for consulting, I hope you consider fair fees that work for all as the foundation of just engagements.

## When the Work Is Done

I believe in the power of ending well. When my kids were little and they understandably didn't want to leave someplace fun, I would tell them, "If you make it easy to leave, you make it easy to come back." When we complete our engagements and processes well, it creates ease for us to move on well to the next thing. Ending well includes taking time to acknowledge, celebrate, and appreciate what we have accomplished.

Our work is done when we agree that we have met our desired outcomes. As we proceed with our work, I regularly remind my client where we are in the process and what we agreed would constitute the final product. I do this because it is surprisingly easy to lose track. As on a sailing trip, once we leave land, it can be hard to see where we have come from and where we are going. These ongoing check-ins mean there will be no surprises at the end. We both know where we're headed, where we are at any single point in the journey, and what more we need to do reach our goal.

When I believe an engagement is complete, I always confirm with the client to make sure that we've met our expectations. If we haven't — or we disagree, though this rarely happens — we need to understand why and what else we need to do. We fully conclude the engagement only when we agree that it is complete; an agreement that includes determining what we achieved and understanding together why our process or desired outcomes shifted, if that's what happened.

This agreement can be part of the formal closure I have with clients at the end of each engagement, usually in the form of a conversation. The client reflects on where they are and what they have learned, we make sure they are clear about their next steps, and I learn what worked well and what I could do better or differently to serve them and other clients in the future. Depending upon the needs of the client, I sometimes write a final summary detailing the engagement's process, products, and key lessons.

I never want clients to become dependent on me; I am helping them build their own capacity. At the same time, it is an honor to have long-term clients who know how to use me well, when and where they need me: when they have a new thorny issue; need a new plan or capacity; or face a conflict where I can give them a hand.

I have worked with Livvy and her organization on and off for over ten years. She called recently and said, "We're starting a big new project and are having trouble clarifying our roles. Could you come and facilitate a conversation about roles for me, Kathy, and Ahmed?"

I am delighted to be used in this way: I can give them what they need in the moment because our longstanding relationship enables me to get up to speed quickly.

The ending of an engagement is an occasion for celebration and reflection that gives us energy to move into what's next. While the engagement may be over, often the relationship continues. Ending well sets the stage for me to continue to be a resource.

# Beginning an Engagement

*The best time to plant a tree was 20 years ago. The second-best time is today.*
— Origin unknown, often attributed
as a "Chinese Proverb."

As an acupuncturist, I determined a course of treatment — which points to needle, what auxiliary therapies and remedies to give, what kind of lifestyle changes to suggest — based on a differential diagnosis. I interviewed my patients to find out who they were, what was happening with them, what symptoms they were experiencing, and what factors in their lives contributed to their well-being and illness. I learned to gather information about the relative health of people's bodies by feeling their pulses, looking at their tongues, palpating their abdomens, and most especially by listening to their stories.

When I enter a system as a consultant, my primary goal is to build trust and relationship. I also need a differential diagnosis to determine the necessary and appropriate interventions. It is easy to jump to conclusions about what is happening, but this generally isn't useful. Lifting the hood to see what's inside can be overwhelming in small systems and organizations, let alone larger and more complex ones, but it is essential. Each system is unique, though we often see predictable patterns.

I have found that the best way to enter a consulting engagement is with a curious mind and an open heart. I seek to learn without judgment or pre-conceived ideas about a system so I can understand their current condition, their hopes and dreams, and where their obstacles and challenges lie. This approach requires a fair amount of vulnerability and courage to resist the temptation to prematurely think I know what to do.

This chapter explores how to enter and build consulting relationships with client organizations, including learning about the system and building trust.

## Who Is the Client?

I always have a primary client within the system. This is usually the person who hired me and the main person to whom I am accountable. They are almost always a decision-maker in a formal leadership position: executive director, board chair, department head, etc. As gatekeepers whose blessing is required to implement change, their support is critical to the technical success of our engagement. At the same time, the relationship and trust we build are critical to setting the stage for a transformational process grounded in love and justice.

What I am really invested in, however, is the system itself. This is the organization, team, or group of people who are the focus of my engagement. I am often seen as (and in fact am) an ally for my key client. But it is a delicate dance. I am not there to do anyone's bidding. My primary allegiance is to the system we are seeking to shift. My key client and I need to be very clear that it is my job to support them in service of our shared values and the well-being of the whole system, but not for their personal goals or needs. If there is a conflict of interest, we need to be able to talk openly about it.

Ultimately, I am an ally to everyone within the system as they work to align individually with the system's highest purpose and values. I need to build as much trust as possible with each of them. Some people will remain suspicious of an outside consultant, no matter how trustworthy I believe myself to be. Regardless, I am committed to listening to everyone.

Ideally, the person leading the work has built support for the initiative before they bring me in and has included others in the decision to hire me. This is very helpful for several reasons. First, when people participate in choosing their consultant, they are more likely to invest in our work together, and I will likely face fewer barriers as I seek to build relationships and trust. Second, when more people in the organization weigh in, the consultant is likely to match more individual needs and interests. And third, transformational work requires sharing power (I will discuss this later on). Sharing the hiring decision creates a model for the work we will do together, which the organization will hopefully carry on into the future.

## Articulate the Process
Thoughtfully constructed processes give people confidence and create trust. Designing processes for predictability and emergence is an art and a science.

Once the consulting engagement is underway, the process can sometimes feel mysterious to the participants. Busy folks can easily lose the thread of where we are. I develop process maps to guide the project and make the work visible. We develop elements of the process map during contracting, but by the time we get into the actual work, we usually need to expand the level of detail.

As with my contracts, I typically situate process maps in the POP framework. As well as Purpose, Outcomes, and Process, we include details about timelines, roles, products, activities, decision-making roles, and stakeholder engagement. The result is a detailed outline of the overall process. While the process map may have much of the same content as the contract, it contains greater process detail and, perhaps most importantly, is a public document to be shared widely. In contrast, contracts tend to be private documents between me and my primary client and include payment agreements.

I generally develop the process map together with my primary client. If a group of people is guiding the process, I further craft and refine the map with them. As the work progresses, I often refer to the map to orient myself and my clients to where we are, what comes next, and what might need to shift.

Just like any good plan, a process map should have the flexibility to shift as we learn new information. Like a contract, a map should only be drawn as far as we can see. It may need to be iterative as we discover more about the system, and we need to leave room for processes to adapt if needed. It is much easier to draw maps for processes with a generally predictable arc (e.g., strategic planning) than more emergent and messier processes (e.g., culture change).

My colleague and I were facilitating a strategic planning process with Healthy Futures Here, a health advocacy organization. We worked with the ED, Patrice, and the board chair, Paloma, to build a representative planning committee to hold the process. Midway into the process, the committee felt things were going well. However, external pressures were putting extra demands on the board, staff, and organization as a whole. Together with Patrice, Paloma and the planning committee, we agreed to slow down the process so as not to further burden people who were already over-taxed. This proved to be a good decision — people were energized by the planning and appreciated the slow pace of the process.

When we made this decision, we had already held three virtual board and staff mini-retreats filled with connection, creativity, and generative conversations; completed a SWOT (Strengths, Weaknesses, Opportunities, and Threats) analysis; and were in the process of finishing up organizational values. Already HFH had learned a lot about its work, external environment, core beliefs, and possible future directions.

Next up, we had planned to continue with Mission and Vision before doing a Strategy Filter (see Tools and Resources). We considered the pace at which the process was moving as we looked over the process map. We noticed that a Strategy Filter would be an immediately helpful tool, so we proposed to Patrice and Paloma that we flip the order and do it next. They were entirely on board.

Shifting in this way turned out to be an excellent move. Creating the Strategy Filter was, as we had hoped, both energizing and immediately useful, both as a long-term tool and for many of the decisions they currently faced. When we returned to the more abstract Mission and Vision, we had even more clarity about the organization.

Using the process map as a living guide enabled us to refine the process so that it was as relevant and valuable to our clients as possible.

Here's my process map template. You'll see the POP framework at work!

I. Purpose, Desired Outcomes, and Assumptions

*Purpose:*

*Desired Outcomes:*

*Assumptions on which this Process Map is based:*

## II. Roles and Responsibilities

*The roles and responsibilities of the* **Strategic Planning Committee** *will be:*

*The roles and responsibilities of the* **Internal Leader** *will be:*

*The roles and responsibilities of the* **board** *and other stakeholders will be:*

*The roles and responsibilities of the* **consultant** *will be:*

## III. Tasks, Roles and Timeline

| TIMEFRAME When will this happen? | TASK What will we do? (e.g. board / staff retreat)? | DELIVERABLE What will we have as a result? (e.g. draft organizational values) | ROLES Who will be involved & what will they do? (e.g. board & staff participate, consultant plan & facilitate) |
|---|---|---|---|
| | | | |

Clearly articulated process maps foster inclusion as people can know what to expect and when. They also promote accountability to a rewarding process with successful results.

## Assemble Champions

Q: *How many consultants does it take to change an organization?*

A: *One, but the organization has to really want to change.*

— Variation on an old joke

Many leaders and systems want consultants to assume full responsibility for their engagements, from the success of the process to the results. This can be super tempting for me, as I care about the work and I want it to go well. However, it's a trap. Transformational consultants can catalyze, facilitate, and hold space for change. But despite the old lightbulb joke, people in the organization need to hold responsibility for the changes in order for real and sustained transformation to take root.

As a consultant, I'm a guest in the organization. My outsider stance enhances my insight into what they need but can also hamper it. While my external perspective contributes significantly to the work, organizations need solutions rooted in what will work for *them*. Equally important, the people who will carry the solutions and directions forward must champion the work, or they are unlikely to succeed in the long run. When processes get challenging, outside consultants can be an easy scapegoat. Conversely, progress is more likely to endure if the will and conviction to embrace and sustain change live inside the organization and are ultimately held by many people.

When my clients are overwhelmed, don't know how to do something, or could use a hand, it is tempting to take on tasks that are their responsibility. They have hired me to help them, and I want to help, but when I help with things outside the scope of what I have agreed to do, it rarely works out well. When I do their work, it keeps them from participating in the system of commitment and responsibility we have put together for the effort and thereby undermines its potential success. For transformational change to take root and persist, internal leadership must own the responsibility.

I have found it more effective to partner with my clients to hold responsibility for the success of the work together from the beginning. This usually involves assembling a small team whose name varies depending on what we are doing: Planning Committee, Retreat Committee, Strategic Alignment Committee, Steering Committee, Culture Change Committee. I think of these teams as the starting point for a ripple of trust and the will to change to spread within the organization. From a place of increasing trust, we can think together about what the system needs.

The committee needs to have a clear mandate and understand the outcome they seek. It may be a successful retreat, a plan for the organization, or guidance for a long-term change effort within the system. The mandate usually comes from the primary client. These leaders may belong to the committee or delegate to it. Sometimes the committee is charged with developing its own mandate.

I've worked with committees that met once or twice to plan time-limited events like retreats. At the other extreme are committees that have met for years to support ongoing initiatives. It is not unusual for folks to tell me how important and even life-changing these committees have been. It may be the first time they have belonged to a group that has listened carefully, built trust, and sorted through hard and important issues. It is always my hope that wherever people go next, they will bring with them the skills and ways of being they learned in these committees.

When people ask who should be on the committee, I generally recommend including:

- People who represent divergent perspectives and identities within the organization
- People who have tolerance for processes and meetings
- People who are trusted and have credibility so that the process itself is seen as credible and trusted
- People who can hold the well-being of the whole and not just represent their own interests

These people bring wisdom from different parts of the system. I can't possibly know all the system's contours and considerations, but together they do. My primary client usually coordinates and leads the group. My role is to facilitate and guide, ask questions and probe, and rigorously hold them to their goals with compassion and care, while being mindful of supporting the leadership and voice of all participants.

It is especially important that the leader be clear about how power lives within the group and how decisions will be made. Will the group advise them? Strive for consensus? Make a recommendation to a final decision-maker (e.g., the Board of Directors, CEO)?

Some people fear that power differentials in these groups will inhibit their work. Sometimes they do. But at the same time, when final decision-makers are not in the room, the group's decisions and recommendations are more easily ignored. When we build trust and support people with positional power to learn to truly listen, power differentials become less of a barrier.

Building shared power and responsibility for the work's success is an important ingredient in creating sustained transformation. I make it explicitly clear that this is one aim of our engagement. It is amazing to see groups empower themselves and take ownership. I have seen many people rise in their leadership and shine in new and beautiful ways through being a part of these groups.

## Discovery and Assessment

Although I learn as much as possible about the client during the contracting phase, once the engagement begins, there is usually more to learn about the system's condition and current issues. This phase is called Discovery. It's usually an iterative process as the organization and I get to know each other.

During Discovery, I generally conduct some kind of an assessment. Organizational assessments reveal a fuller picture of the whole system to those within it. Seeing their story together and finding truths we can agree on — even if we can only agree that we all see this situation differently — creates a foundational energy of alignment and a basis for forward movement. This is particularly important for change processes.

During Discovery, I have to resist the impulse to move quickly or be swayed by a compelling leader's analysis. Instead,

I need to slow down long enough to get a full picture of the current condition and take the time to listen and learn as much as I can about the system. To embody justice, we must pay close attention to the voices and perspectives of people who have less positional power, historically excluded identities, or both.

The breadth of the assessment depends on the scope of the work. For an organizational change effort, we'll want to reach out as widely as we can. For a team building retreat, we may just want to hear from members of the team.

Assessments can look at:

- Structures
- Operations
- Culture
- Equity, inclusion, racism, and other forms of oppression
- Leadership
- Management of resources
- The general condition of the organization

It is also helpful to learn what other processes clients are currently engaged in or might be planning. While I generally ask upfront about other organizational activities and initiatives, clients may not realize that culture, branding, and finance, for instance, may be relevant to our work.

Information for assessments can be gathered from:

- Interviews with key stakeholders (staff, board, customers, clients, students, members)
- Surveys of key stakeholders
- Focus groups or facilitated conversations with key stakeholders
- Observations (meetings, physical locations, programs, etc.)
- Participant co-interviews (in which participants gather information from each other)

- Document reviews (e.g., annual reports, financial statements, strategic plans)

When I do an assessment, I need to be careful not to fall into confirmation bias — seeing and gathering only data that confirms what I already think. Instead, I need to look as broadly as I can. As with everything in this human realm, assessments show only partial truth; there is always more to learn.

I love the idea of "inquiry as intervention," which I learned from the consulting group Essential Partners. It holds that the way we ask questions and enter a system IS an intervention. The system can begin shifting even before the t's are crossed and i's are dotted in an assessment. We are already building relationships by asking questions and raising the possibility of new and different ways of seeing ourselves and understanding our work. For instance, when I take the time to speak individually with each member of a team in preparation for a retreat, listening carefully and without judgment to their experiences, I am modeling an alternative to the hurried pace that does not allow teams space for real human connection. And the very questions we ask can invite new ways of thinking.

Appreciative Inquiry (AI), developed by David Cooperrider, offers a beautiful and helpful approach to asking questions and framing conversations. AI holds that the seeds of solutions and health are already present within every system, though detritus and distraction often surround them. Since we will always find what we're looking for, if we focus on what's broken, we'll see only brokenness. When we look for what's working and enlivening within an organization, we can use what we find to access pathways for transformation, build the confidence to develop and pursue a new image of the future, and lift the whole system to a better place. AI is not about ignoring difficult truths but rather about seeing them within a context of possibility (see Tools and Resources for more about Appreciative Inquiry).

One of the tenets of organizational change is to "reveal the system to itself." People inside the organization need to understand their context and how the system works through them to understand how to change it. Organizational assessments are mirrors for clients to see themselves. I try to listen carefully and understand the system's condition with a clear eye — and ear — toward painting a picture of their current reality.

Less is usually more in written assessments. It can be tempting to write a comprehensive treatise on everything I've discovered. I've seen the tomes, dense, thick, and filled with data and information, as if the compilation alone will solve the problems at hand. I believe shorter is often better so people can really engage with it.

I strive to present the assessment findings in neutral language, simply stating the facts I have uncovered. If there isn't agreement on specific issues, I note that (e.g., "there is a lack of agreement among the staff about x"). As much as possible, I want people to take in the information without defensiveness or shame. My mantra when writing up assessments is "metabolizability," so I am careful to use non-judgmental language (e.g., "staff do not always have the training they need" rather than "staff are unskilled") and hold compassion in my heart as I write up and present my findings. I strive to hold the truth of human fallibility and struggle with grace and care on the one hand and without pity or apology on the other. This usually helps people allow themselves to see the fuller picture.

It is tempting to include solutions in assessments, especially when obvious ones emerge. However, for the type of collaborative process consulting that I do, it's important to keep the assessment separate from the possible actions it can generate. People need to sit together in the truth of where they are and define the problem before they seek solutions. I often include questions or possibilities for them to consider as they move forward and note contradictions or polarities that may be useful to address. I do sometimes include an appendix with "interesting suggestions" to capture good ideas that emerged during the assessment.

There is a famous parable that's useful when thinking about assessments. It is said to have originated centuries ago in India and originally featured a group of blind people and an elephant. I am grateful to Rachel Tanenhaus from the Cambridge Commission for People with Disabilities, who told me "It's fine to talk about 'seeing' and 'seen' but please don't use blindness as a metaphor." With thanks to my colleague and thought partner, Jeremy Philips, I offer a more inclusive revision of this parable.

The story goes that a group of people learn that there is a mysterious creature in the woods just outside their village. It is pitch black outside, and they have no source of light. They go together to the woods to find out more about the creature. One person places their hands on the elephant's leg. "The creature is a pillar," they announce. Another touches the ears. "No, the creature is a fan," they proclaim. Yet another feels the trunk and insists, "The creature is a hose." And still another grabs the tail and declares, "This creature is a rope."

When we are inside organizations, we usually know only the piece of the elephant that we are holding, and we believe that the whole system is what we can "see." Even people who have a more comprehensive view of the system, such as top executives, are often unaware of large parts of what is present, or absent, in the organization. Coming to a shared understanding can be easy and quick, or complicated and emotional.

When people hold different understandings of the current state, it's hard to create alignment and clarity about how to move. As with most things in organizational consulting, it all depends on what's present in the system. If I present a mirror, are people willing to look fully at who they are, how they're behaving, and what's true about their context?

I see asking people about their experiences and opinions as a kind of commitment. Once I am entrusted with the data, I must hold it with care and share what I've learned with all involved. When people within the system hear their story carefully told by an outsider, it is usually a relief, though there can also be grief and sadness. In systems with a lot of pain, this is an opportunity for empathy and compassion.

"We're really in a mess," Beth said during our first call. "We don't know what to do!" She was on the board of Darn Good, a US non-profit partnering with women worldwide to repair and refurbish clothing.

"We just had to fire our ED. He was terribly incompetent and saw things very differently than the board. He didn't care at all about our producer partners! But now, the board is at each other's throats! We can't agree at all on what to do. We think we may need to dissolve the organization. That would be tragic. The women we partner with count on us, and we make great stuff that people love."

I listened through her palpable pain as Beth described a very confusing situation. She had been on the board for five years and cared a lot about the organization. For nearly an hour, she talked about the personalities involved, numerous disputes, and a minor PR scandal.

"It sounds like a lot is going on, and it's not yet clear where exactly to begin," I said. "How about if I do an assessment and write a brief summary of the issues and possible ways to move forward?"

"That's perfect," Beth said, "exactly what we need." Beth spoke with the other executive committee members who agreed to a plan that included a facilitated session with the executive committee to develop a recommendation to the board for moving forward.

As I conducted 1:1 interviews with the 12 members of the board and the 5 remaining staff people, a clear and consistent picture emerged. I captured what I'd heard in a short report.

The members of the executive committee were greatly relieved to see my assessment. It helped them all to step outside the screen of their current pain and resentment and see Darn Good more clearly. I held up the organization's great strengths and many assets — trusted partnerships with their producers and customers, a track record of great creativity, skilled staff, loyal funders, and committed board members. I also acknowledged their current difficulties, which boiled down to a lack of clarity about their values, vision, and strategic directions; some shame about the mess they were in; and a lot of fear about what might happen if they didn't get it together. I recommended that the board and staff gather for an in-person retreat, and they eagerly agreed.

The assessment opened a doorway for Darn Good to enter into a process of intensive soul searching and new ways of thinking, which resulted in passionate recommitment to the organization and its future success.

I've learned the hard way that it's important to help leaders understand that the assessment is likely to reflect their own challenges and weaknesses as well as the organization's. I haven't always taken careful time to prepare and support leaders to manage their potential anxiety and defensiveness. But I've learned that this step is critical.

I was approached by Tammy, the founder of Arts and All, a small non-profit community arts organization, to do an organizational assessment. After more than ten years of bootstrapping, Arts and All had grown and the organization had recently hired their first paid executive director, Thomas. Tammy had stepped out of the role of volunteer ED and into the role of president, attending only to public-facing functions and fundraising. Thomas now ran the organization.

The new structure had been in place for almost a year, and things weren't going well. Projects were stalled and tensions were rising. The board was uncertain about what to do. Had they made a mistake in hiring Thomas? Thomas, Tammy, and the board agreed to hire me to do a brief assessment to get a picture of what was happening.

Speaking individually with Tammy, Thomas, the two other staff members, and several board members, I heard a straightforward story. Everyone loved Tammy. She was a hero in the community and had created an exciting and beloved organization. With trepidation and sadness, many also reported that she was creating all kinds of difficulty in her new role. She had not let go of any control or power, which was hampering Thomas's ability to make decisions and move things forward. Tammy questioned his actions at every turn, publicly and with the board. The board was confused and unsure what to do.

I captured these challenges in a brief report. Before sending the assessment to the board, I arranged to meet privately with both Thomas and Tammy and then with Eliza, the board chair. I met first with Thomas to ensure that I had accurately represented his input. "I'm so relieved," Thomas said when he saw his experience reflected in my report. Next, I met with Tammy. We reviewed what I had found. Despite all my care and attention to neutral and non-blaming language, she was furious and denied that her behavior was in any way part of the problem. In hindsight, I can see that she was also ashamed.

Before doing the assessment, I should have sat with Tammy and helped her understand that a leader's behavior and choices always impact the health of their organization. I also should have explained that Founder's Syndrome — the common and understandable difficulty founders can have in turning their "baby" over to others — was at play here.

If I had helped Tammy understand this phenomenon before she saw the assessment, she might have been able to understand the role she played in the organization's current circumstances differently. Instead, she was incensed and felt betrayed by the board and staff. Though she didn't say it, I believe she felt betrayed by me as well. Over the next year, a power struggle ensued, and Tammy ultimately forced Thomas out.

This experience taught me to always take time and care to prepare leaders for the likelihood that an assessment will reveal things about them that may be hard to hear. And I always process assessments with leaders privately before presenting them to a broader group.

I find that these initial assessments can inform my work with an organization for many years to come. As a snapshot of a moment in time that we can use as an ongoing reference, an assessment helps me notice progress and change or highlight persistent issues.

It's important that we model transformational and just values, care, compassion, and equity in the ways we set up and begin our work with clients; how we begin an engagement sets the stage for everything that can come afterwards.

# We Shape Systems as Systems Shape Us

*Whatever is inside of us continually flows outward, helping to form or deform the world — depending on what we send out. Whatever is outside us continually flows inward, helping to form or deform us — depending on how we take it in.*

— Parker Palmer

As I enter a new system or work with a system over time, I need to be aware of the forces at play — the things that are impacting and influencing the system — to understand what is happening and what kinds of interventions may be needed. If a giant wall in the way is invisible to me, I will likely crash right into it.

People create systems, and systems work through people. We are collectively what keeps systems in place. When we more clearly understand the forces that shape our systems and the interplay between us and our systems, and we ground ourselves in our values and our vision of the world we want to create, we can begin to re-shape our systems so that we can work more effectively toward creating that world.

This chapter is about naming, recognizing, and understanding primary forces that shape and impact my client organizations. These include racism and systemic oppression, mental models, power, and culture. The subsequent chapters will address how we navigate these forces to facilitate transformational change.

## Racism and Systemic Oppression

Racism is everywhere, in the air we breathe and the water we drink, causing real harm. The delusional ideology of racism wants us to believe that racialized hierarchy, like air and water, is natural. But race is a human-invented construct. As long as we do racism's bidding, treating this lie as truth and allowing it to influence our decisions and our actions, its harm to people and the planet will continue to be real.

The impact of racism and systemic oppression is present in all organizations in overt and covert ways. We see it in who gets hired, who is included in decision-making, who is promoted, who confides in whom, who is given the benefit of the doubt, and who is trusted. Racism and systemic oppression inform and impact the work organizations do, the services they provide, the resources they secure, and how they use those resources.

I once worked at an organization where the executive director was a white man, all the mid-managers were white women (including me), and the one Black employee was the administrative assistant. It had just "happened" that way, as it does in many predominantly white organizations. When people and organizations are not mindful of the dynamics of racism and systemic oppression, racialized patterns of power and access to resources will recreate themselves.

It is incumbent on consultants of all identities to have a critical analysis about the dynamics of racism and systemic oppression so we can understand when we encounter them and how to contradict them as we do our work.

People, mostly white, sometimes ask me why we should focus on racism in Diversity, Equity, and Inclusion (DEI) work. They point out the many ways that humans are excluded and oppressed based on identity: sexism, homophobia, transphobia, ableism, ageism, antisemitism, Islamophobia, fatphobia, xenophobia, heightism, and more. These oppressions are real and have harmful impacts.

As a short-statured Jewish woman, I can experience people questioning my worth as a human being subtly and overtly.

So why center racism, particularly anti-Black racism? Because it is the nexus of this country's toxicity of othering and dehumanization. The US was established on the principle that some humans deserve resources, respect, and autonomy while others do not. This fundamental belief engendered slavery, genocide, and the theft of land and labor. It is the principle that drives our extractive capitalist economy and the foundational ideology that allows and encourages the perpetuation of all our other oppressions.

Racism is also a prime barrier to creating organizations and systems rooted in love. It is a cornerstone that holds all injustice in place. Unlearning racism is a reclamation of humanity, both for people targeted by its brutal impact and for those of us socialized to maintain its cruelty.

These pernicious forces are not easily undone, and I believe it will be the work of generations. This is our time on the planet, the baton is now in our hands. If we truly wish to do transformational work in organizations and in the world, working against racism is not optional.

## Mental Models and Mistaken Facticity

*We're walking around inside of someone else's imagination of how this world could work.*

— adrienne maree brown

I first learned about mental models from Peter Senge's seminal book, *The 5th Discipline*. Mental models are our beliefs about how the world works; they form the basis for all our actions. We usually aren't even aware of them, but they drive everything we do. They come from our personal histories, cultures, and other factors that shape us, like religious upbringing, education, and social milieu. For example, I grew up in a house built in the 1800s. My parents liked older things and passed on to me a belief that older construction is always better than new. Hence, I bought a house built in 1893, despite all the problems with older homes and the many beautiful newer houses. This is my mental model at work!

In graduate school, I learned the useful construct of mistaken facticity: believing something is a fact when it is not. Mistaken facticity also drives our behaviors, policies, and practices, which makes it a sibling to mental models. This notion has been very useful in both my personal life and my work. For example, I might have mistaken facticity about how much I can get done on a Saturday morning: water the garden, clean my house, shop for groceries, cook a meal for a sick neighbor, AND walk with a friend?!? My mistaken facticity leads me to plan for what I can't possibly accomplish, which keeps me out of integrity and alignment. It also has a real impact when I have to call my friend at the last minute and explain that the morning got away from me and I don't have time for our walk. Mistaken facticity can undermine trust, relationships, and efficacy on both personal and organizational levels.

Our own mental models and mistaken facticity are powerful forces that distort how we see the world and ourselves in it. They make the conclusions we draw on the basis of inevitably partial and limited data, appear to us not just as reality but as ironclad truth. We build our choices, actions, and organizational strategies from our collective mental models, even as they may be chock-full of mistaken facticity. Helping systems and individuals to understand and reckon with their mental models and mistaken facticity that keep the status quo in place is central to transformational consulting.

We bring our mental models and mistaken facticity to work with us. They are always at play and can keep individuals and organizations, even those who espouse commitments to social justice, operating in ways that continue to replicate harm. Unexamined mental models allow us to uphold policies and practices that allocate resources to those with privilege and continue to deny them to historically excluded folks. People often think they have no option but to adhere to these norms, which lets them continue to perpetuate a false hierarchy of human value based on identity and prioritize the needs and voices of the traditionally dominant.

Our limited human capacity to take in and make meaning of the world around us allows only partial access to the full story of anything. In order to process our environment's vast amounts of data and stimulation, our brains limit us from taking in new information about things we think we know, the stimulation we've become accustomed to, or things we can't process. Like when you stop noticing the familiar sounds of traffic outside your apartment.

This is why helping people to "widen their aperture," to quote Joyce Shabazz, is so critical to changing systems. As consultants, we need to invite people to examine their mental models and the limits of their imagination about what is possible, and it can sometimes be a heavy lift. As humans, we don't tend to shift our mental models easily. Even when confronted with evidence to the contrary, many of us still will not budge from our previous beliefs. But coaching and group learning that helps leaders see and understand their mistaken facticity and limiting mental models can be life-changing for leaders and their organizations.

These explorations need to be held with rigor, love, compassion, and truth so people feel safe enough to see how they have limited their own awareness. As consultants and coaches we cannot do it for them, but we can accompany them on the journey.

Dahlia was a long-time program director for Serving Now, a national hunger relief organization. I had coached her on and off for several years. She was seen as very capable and a bright star within the organization. A year earlier, upon the retirement of the former ED, Dahlia had accepted the role.

She was quickly overworked and overwhelmed in her new position. She felt perpetually behind, spending her time "putting out fires," as she explained during a check-in with me. She could never make time or space to attend to building systems or supports that could prevent many of the fires in the first place. She was frustrated and exhausted. I could hear the anxiety in her voice when she spoke, and I missed seeing the perpetual smile she wore as a program director.

Dahlia asked me to help her figure out how to make her job sustainable. She loved the organization and wanted to do a good job. But at the end of each day, she only felt a sense of failure. I asked her to tell me about all the responsibilities on her plate. As I listened, I noticed that she was very involved with programs and service delivery. She spent a lot of time troubleshooting large and small problems within the organization and attending to programmatic details. She participated in many program-level meetings. If staff needed a hand, she was always available.

I reflected this back to her and asked her if she believed in her staff and thought they could do their jobs. She replied with an emphatic "Yes!" Did she think they had enough staff to deliver services? Again, "yes!" As I continued to ask her questions and listen to her, a pattern emerged, grounded in her mental models.

As Dahlia had risen in her leadership role, she believed herself to be most valuable doing what she knew how to do: delivering programs and managing on the ground. She wanted to be seen as a valuable ED and thought that could only happen if she continued to be closely involved in service delivery.

Her mental model of what she needed to do to be useful meant she couldn't let go of her earlier role. She wasn't doing what she needed to do to succeed: attending to the overall vision and health of the organization and mentoring her staff to grow their skills and rise in their leadership. She had created a dependency that appeared necessary and made her seem indispensable, but not in the way she needed to be in her new role.

The organization desperately needed her to attend to big picture issues: fundraising, long-term planning, clarifying roles and responsibilities, and connecting with others outside the organization. As we constructed the picture together, she saw how she and the organization were suffering. She saw herself only as providing value if she was doing and delivering and could not see that she could lead in another way.

In our coaching I held Dahlia in an inquiry process so she could understand what she was doing, why she was doing it, and the impact of her choices. Dahlia realized that she had been keeping herself stuck in a cycle of overwhelm and enabling, rather than growing her leadership to a new level and thus allowing others to do the same.

### Power

*Power without love is reckless and abusive, and love without power is sentimental and anemic. Power at its best is love implementing the demands of justice, and justice at its best is power correcting everything that stands against love.*

— Martin Luther King Jr.

Alicia Garza defines power as "The ability to make decisions that affect your own life and the lives of others, the freedom to shape and determine the story of who we are. Power also means having the ability to reward and punish and decide how resources are distributed." Power is the force to make things happen — large things, small things, and everything in between. Like fire, power is not inherently good or bad. Rather, how we apply it determines whether it is constructive or destructive.

The confusion, misapplication, and abuse of power causes significant dysfunction and harm in organizations and in the world. This shows up in how individuals hold their power and the structures and processes through which power operates.

Power in organizations can be both formal (designated to specific roles) and informal (based on ability to influence and mobilize). People at all levels of designated authority have informal power that rests in their relationship to personal power and cultural and social forces (e.g., what voices have greater credence based on identity).

I see people in organizations misapply and misunderstand power in four primary ways. Knowing these patterns enables me to recognize and help my clients to see how they may be exercising power in ways that recreate oppression and dysfunction, regardless of their good intentions.

I. *Disavowal of Power,* as named and described by Heather Laine Talley in her blog post: "White Women Doing White Supremacy in Nonprofit Culture," is "regularly denying/ignoring/downplaying how much power we hold."

Like many other people with progressive values (e.g., solidarity, sustainability, equity), I have sometimes conflated power with oppression, understanding oppression to be the inevitable result of power. We often ground this conclusion in historical analysis and personal experience. I see brilliant leaders reluctant to hold the fullness of their power for fear of becoming oppressive. This can be true for people at all levels of positional power within organizations, but it is a posture that does not support effective leadership.

Organizations sometimes pretend that they have no power structure and everyone has equal power all the time. This is almost never true.

It is common to see people socialized as women disavow their power. However, despite our denials, power is always present, especially for white women who have racialized power. When we pretend we don't have it, we can wield it recklessly.

Common expressions and consequences of Disavowal of Power are:

- Not interrupting harm as it's happening
- Not acting when action is needed
- Not holding others accountable for their behaviors or deliverables
- Randomly swooping in and taking over situations from others, depriving them of opportunities to grow in their power
- Setting others up to fail by pretending they have power that they do not have
- Not mentoring others to develop their leadership and power

Amoretta Morris of the Annie E. Casey Foundation writes about "Liberated Gatekeepers." She explains that "Gatekeepers, after all, control the flow of power, funds, information and resources." When we deny power, we cannot act as liberated gatekeepers: by not opening the doors to which we hold the keys, we end up denying others access to power. I support my clients to tell the truth about where power lies and claim their own power.

II. *Power Over.* This is the prevailing model of power in our culture and could also be called authoritarian power. Based on dominance ideology, it is the mistaken notion that power is a zero-sum game and if someone has power, someone else cannot have it. In this model, power is only for the few, and people with power know better than others. Everyone else needs to come in line and be kept in line.

I continually see people default to Power Over, even when they aspire to something different, because the model is ingrained in us. It's hard for us to imagine other options, particularly when we are stressed. Without mindfully interrupting patterns, shifting our mental models, and figuring out how to operate outside of dominance, we are likely to revert to this way of being.

Common expressions of and consequences of Power Over are:

- Re-creation of dominance and subjugation based on identity (e.g., racism, sexism, etc.)
- Disenfranchised, demoralized, de-energized, exhausted, and overburdened staff
- Thwarted innovation and creativity
- Neglected stakeholders, as people with positional authority lose touch with their needs
- Negative impacts on mental and physical health
- Inequitable distribution of resources and access

Non-profit boards are places where people often get confused and apply Power Over. Even in organizations with progressive values, I sometimes see boards acting in dominant ways relative to executive directors and staff. Their positional authority can make boards believe they need to hold all the power and make all the critical decisions.

III. *Power Under* is the flip side of Power Over. It still operates on a model of dominance and subjugation, winners and losers. However, in this case, people cede their power, whether they are asked to or not.

The impact and shame of trauma and systemic oppression can disconnect us from our internal resources and power. Without realizing it, we can cede our power to others, whether or not they have tried to take it from us.

Often, people believe they have no power and behave accordingly, but the truth is more complicated. Institutions and society curtail power but believing that they lack power can cut people off from available opportunities to own power and influence.

Common expressions and consequences of Power Under are:

- Not speaking the truth or speaking up
- Not letting people know one's real needs
- Disconnection from one's voice and wisdom
- Withholding wisdom and creativity
- Loss of energy
- Harm to physical, emotional, and mental well-being

IV. *Covert Power* is pretending not to have power while exerting control. It is often labeled passive-aggressive. I recently heard the great phrase "hiding knives in your words." Covert power can take up all the space in a room while pretending it's coming from a powerless place.

Common expressions and consequences of Covert Power are:

- Subtle bullying
- Sabotage
- Psychological harm
- Fraying of trust and authenticity in relationships
- Stifled growth and creativity
- Fear
- Anger

A Way Forward: *Power With*
Power With is the understanding that power is not a zero-sum game and that some people having power does not mean that others won't also. When people practice "power with," they own their power and strive to act in ways that does not diminish the power of others. Recognizing power dynamics related to identity, position, and personal leadership in groups and relationships, they stand in their power to create liberation, leadership, and access for others. This type of power creates trust and could be called "authoritative."

Some expressions and consequences of Power With are:

- Organizational structures that share power and decision-making more broadly, rather than concentrating it at the top, and create "leader-full" organizations where wisdom and the power to implement effective actions are distributed throughout the system
- Institutional practices for noticing who is — and isn't — at the table and expanding opportunities for participation in decision-making (where possible and appropriate)
- Sharing resources and opportunities rather than hoarding them
- Making sure people have clear expectations for success and the information and resources they need, then trusting them to make good decisions
- Equitable distribution of salaries and other resources
- Honest acknowledgment of where power lies in any given situation

Power With doesn't mean that hierarchies and levels of accountability cease to exist. It means that everyone in the organization is mindful of how power operates. Those with power, especially those with the most power, need to be the most committed to being open and inclusive about its workings.

Two important practices to counteract Power Over and create Power With are: (1) creating an authentic partnership between people who occupy different levels of positional power and; (2) bringing people together across perceived lines of positional power (e.g., board and staff) to think creatively about specific issues or future directions.

Through coaching and group learning, I strive to help my clients to come into honest and effective relationship with power. This is usually profoundly personal work for people at all levels of positional power. It involves unpacking mental models, personal histories, beliefs around power, and internalized messages about social locations and how different kinds of people are expected to be in a relationship with power. It can be liberating to understand and begin to contradict the messages we receive from racism and patriarchy about who is entitled to own their power and the roles different identities are expected to play in relation to power.

Humans are complex beings. We can experience and manifest power in many different ways in a single day or even hour. It takes lifelong commitment and ongoing practice to grow ever more aware of the impact of how we hold power. As we strive to build more just organizations, consultants need to continually shine a light on how people are applying power.

## Culture

*It's funny how much our surroundings influence our emotions. Our joys and sorrows, likes and dislikes are colored by our environment so much that often we just let our surroundings dictate our course. We go along with "public" feelings until we no longer even know our own true aspirations. We become a stranger to ourselves, molded entirely by society...*

— Thich Nhat Hanh

*You think you are thinking your thoughts, you are not; you are thinking the culture's thoughts.*

— Jiddu Krishnamurti

Organizational culture is the (generally unstated) context, including norms and mores, that tells people how they are supposed to be in a system. It frames everything within an organization: how people treat each other, what behaviors are expected and rewarded, what gets celebrated, who gets valued, and what behaviors are penalized. People new to organizations can spend a lot of time and energy trying to decode the culture, particularly when their identities differ from the dominant identities within the organization.

Some examples of organizational culture include:

- How people communicate with each other, verbally and otherwise (e.g., expectations about how quickly to return emails, whether or not to chat in the hallways)
- What is and isn't okay to talk about (e.g., emotions, racism and oppression)
- How people behave and comport themselves (e.g., what clothes are acceptable, how loudly — or softly — people are expected to speak, how much emotion is shown)
- The ways that people work together (e.g., collaboratively, competitively)
- The types of people and accomplishments seen as "successful" (e.g., who receives public recognition outside of the organization or is celebrated when they achieve goals)
- How people get developed and promoted (e.g., mentoring)
- Organizational "traditions" (e.g., celebrations, recognition of significant life events)
- The "material" environment (e.g., what kind of space people work in, how it is decorated, what kind of food is available, what kind of art or whose pictures are on the wall)
- How people are held accountable to each other and their work (e.g., performance reviews, how and when feedback is given and received)
- How conflict and dissent are managed (e.g., use of restorative practices that build communication and understanding and seek to repair harm, avoidance of open conflict)

Organizational culture impacts:

- Who feels welcome and like they belong in the organization

- Who feels safe to be their full self at work and who feels like they need to hide parts of themself or their identity
- Who gets the benefit of the doubt in complicated situations or when they make a mistake
- The health and well-being (physical, emotional, and spiritual) of everyone inside the organization
- The way work gets done, and in particular whether it is in alignment with organizational values
- Morale, job satisfaction, and retention
- Creativity and innovation
- The quality of the organization's work

Culture is learned and contagious; we usually catch and spread it without awareness. That said, knowing and satisfactorily performing culture tends to be a source of informal organizational power.

"Culture eats strategy for breakfast" is a common consulting refrain. This extends to lunch and dinner as well. Organizational culture dictates what behavior is acceptable and rewarded. It impacts how people use their time and what parts of themselves they access while at work. You can have all the strategies, policies, and rhetoric in the world, but ultimately people will behave in ways dictated by culture.

Factors outside of organizations also influence their culture. I believe it's impossible to operate fully outside the dominant culture. The ubiquitous impact of racism and other oppressions do not wait outside the organization's door. The impact of societal norms is always present.

Within a short time, everyone who enters an organization is impacted by its culture. Many become part of the forcefield that holds the culture in place, whether they believe in it or not, whether it is serving them or not. Some may fully endorse the culture. Others may support the culture in public or when leaders and supervisors are around while also creating protective subcultures with small groups of colleagues. Others may challenge the culture.

How dissenters are seen — held up as heroic and helpful or used as cautionary tales — becomes part of the organization's cultural narrative. Significant gaps between an organization's internal culture and the rhetoric and images it projects to outside stakeholders often land as hypocritical with staff, undermining trust and damaging the cultural narrative.

Fostering a healthy culture builds organizational effectiveness and efficiency. The most effective organizational cultures I've seen foster a sense of belonging, purpose, and accountability. Cultivating culture is not a one-time event but an ongoing process of care and tending.

Shifting culture is perhaps the hardest thing to do. The prevailing wisdom that organizational culture change efforts require a minimum of three years to take hold accords with my experience. We develop muscle memory for behaving within a culture. Even if people fully believe in a different way of being, they often continue to accommodate and respond to the existing culture.

Culture change cannot be dictated from the "top," but paradoxically, it is nearly impossible to shift without the real engagement of top leadership. To sustain, culture change has to be institutionalized. Just as organizational culture (and particularly its harmful aspects) persists beyond the tenure of individuals, I have seen progress crumble when change efforts are dependent on leaders who leave the organization.

People for Care, a small health advocacy non-profit with an entirely white staff, was having trouble. The executive director, Bonnie, a long-time staff member, had been promoted to her role almost two years earlier. Through some previous work I had done with People For Care, Bonnie and I had developed a good trusting relationship.

She truly wanted to do whatever she could to succeed and help the organization thrive, so she asked me to help her.

"We spend a lot of time 'spinning yarns,'" she told me. "We just don't tell each other the truth about what we're each doing." Follow through was poor, she reported, and collaboration was almost non-existent. "We develop plans, and everyone just does their own thing!" Walking through the People for Care's offices, I could sense the surface politeness that was their overt culture.

We began where I often start culture change efforts, with an assessment of the current condition. I conducted interviews with all staff members and presented the findings to Bonnie. The assessment revealed underlying frustration, dis-ease, and a culture of individualism and privacy.

We agreed to begin with 1:1 leadership coaching for her. Over a few sessions, she understood that the culture was comfortable for her — it was her natural way of being. She saw the mental models that told her being a leader meant always knowing the answers and telling others what to do, asking for help or advice was a sign of weakness, and vulnerability was taboo. She and the organization valued the appearance of productivity above all else, and people were leaving their full humanity at the door.

Bonnie saw clearly that to be successful, People For Care needed to build an authentic collaborative culture. And for that to happen, she would need to shift her mindset and behaviors before she invited her staff to do the same. Through our coaching, she recognized the roots of her beliefs and behaviors in her childhood, educational training, and white dominance culture. Bravely and vulnerably, she slowly shifted her habits and behaviors. Bonnie began to invite others into collaboration and problem-solving, and she increasingly acted as a coach and facilitator rather than telling people what to do.

After several months, Bonnie invited her small staff into a process to build their team's capacity to collaborate and communicate with one another. I facilitated two team retreats where they learned about their leadership and communication styles by sharing stories and using the DiSC behavioral assessment, clarified roles and decision-making using VARCI, and built a shared vision and agreements about how they wanted to work together (see Tools and Resources for more about DiSC and VARCI). They are now beginning to look at how racism and white dominance drive the culture of their still predominantly white organization.

"You pushed our team to bring our humanity into the work," Bonnie told me as we reflected several years later. "We had separated our bodies completely. You challenged us to bring our whole human self. It was so uncomfortable for our team at first. But we stuck with it, and it's pushed us to a new place, personally and professionally. We're now able to speak and hear more of the truth and know how to collaborate and follow through on our commitments. We're still growing and learning to be more effective, and there are so many tangible and positive impacts from the work we've done. People are way more satisfied in their jobs, and our funding increased because of what we've been able to accomplish. This has enabled us to expand our staff and our impact."

Transformational organizational work requires the courage to change cultures that are sometimes beloved and often deeply entrenched. This work requires fortitude, patience, and a long-term commitment.

# 5

# Levers of Change

*We must transform ourselves to transform the world.*
— Grace Lee Boggs

*Transformation is not magic. It's hard work, but it is also doable work.*
— Sonya Renee Taylor

Change is a multibillion-dollar industry. Books, workshops, consultants, therapists; we're all looking to crack the code for creating real and sustained change. The solutions my clients seek for seemingly intractable problems in the world and inside their organizations often require transformational approaches. Transformation is possible when we move beyond the fears, limiting beliefs, erroneous mental models, and mistaken facticity that stand between us and our full humanity, between us and love.

Ron Heifetz describes the difference between technical and adaptive problems and the types of changes they require. Problems we already know how to solve are technical. My kitchen floor is dirty, so I take out the mop and clean it — a simple solution to a technical problem. I don't need to look beyond my existing skills, reconsider how I understand the world, or develop new tools and relationships to change the condition of my floor.

But if my kitchen floor is dirty because my family tracks in mud every day, despite my repeated pleas to wipe their feet, then we have an adaptive problem. To find a solution, our family has to have a real and honest conversation about what respect and agreements mean for us. This conversation may surface other issues: *Why does mom always clean the floor? Why are we recreating oppressive gender norms that our family does not accept?* Perhaps a new solution emerges. Not only will we all take responsibility for wiping our feet, but we will also rotate responsibility for mopping. If this doesn't work, we'll talk about it again. Depending on how we approach it, this very conversation can deepen our connection and enable us to better live our values as a family.

Transformation means a fundamental change in our understanding of ourselves, our relationships with others, and the world around us. Our actions are different because they are rooted in a different perspective than we had before.

Transformational change processes need to happen on two levels at once: individual and systemic. For systems to change, individuals need to build the will to change them. And for individuals to grow and sustain change, we need organizational systems and cultures to transform and support new ways of being and operating. We must attend to individual and collective growth and learning at the very same time.

I wish I had a magic formula for transformation toward justice and love that was guaranteed to work every time. Sadly, no such luck. As consultants, we have many tools, frameworks, and processes that can help catalyze and support transformation. In this chapter I'll share some key levers we can use to facilitate transformational change.

## Careful Pacing

*Change works its way out in ripples. Sometimes you get
to know where they go, and sometimes you don't.*
— Steven Brion-Meisels

On a chilly winter morning in Maine, my friend Alex and I sat on a small beach, watching a beautiful sunrise. The colors were glorious — all different shades of orange and purple. I sat with rapt attention for several minutes, sensing the world's beauty. But I didn't notice any change in the colors or the light. Then I looked down for a moment. When I looked back up, the sky was very different.

Change efforts can be like that sky; if you're looking at them up close from the inside, it can feel like nothing has happened. But when I leave organizations for a while and come back, I can see significant changes. Sometimes we must look away to notice the shift. Some days it's too cloudy to see, but it is still there. And sometimes the sun has already risen; we may miss its spectacular emergence but its light is shining. Once transformation has occurred, it can seem like life has always been this way.

But unlike the sunrise (or the metamorphosis of a caterpillar, another frequent metaphor for change and growth), organizational transformation is not linear. I used to push harder on the pace of unfolding change. I see it! It's possible! Let's make it happen! Now I know that change takes time and happens at its own unpredictable pace.

When I was a kid, we used to make a substance we called Gush Balls. Perhaps you know it as oobleck or by another name. It is simply corn starch with a bit of water, sometimes with food coloring added for pizazz. If you hold the substance lightly in your hands, it melts. If you squeeze it or push on it, it hardens. It's helpful to think of people in change processes as like Gush Balls. If you push them too quickly beyond their capacity to absorb, they harden and there is nowhere else to go. If you hold them without a sturdy container, they melt and lose all shape.

We need to find the pace that is just right — slow enough that everyone can come along and fast enough that we maintain momentum and energy. This especially presents a challenge for visionary leaders who often must learn to slow down to give their people time and space to catch up. People with less positional power and from historically marginalized identities can also be frustrated as initiatives do not make perceptible impacts in their daily lives quickly enough to build trust that change will come.

Change processes pose a significant paradox for individuals and systems. We are asking people to create a future distinct from their current reality, one in which they will be different in some way. Their beliefs might be called into question or their job responsibilities and priorities could shift. And yet, for most of us to let down our defenses toward liberation, we need to feel seen and validated in our humanity, just as we are, before we can let down our defenses and embrace a picture of where we might want to be.

Organizations often misunderstand what transformation entails. They want shortcuts, checklists, and recipes for change. But while there are lots of helpful change techniques, technologies, and training, they don't necessarily take into account the fact that organizations have particular circumstances and needs. When organizations jump to implementing them without sustained commitment and attention to what they truly need, these tools don't usually bring about outcomes that allow for real and sustained transformation.

I try not to overpack my schedule so I can leave room for the needs that emerge as transformations are underway. For an upset or conflict that needs tending, or for unanticipated planning or coaching that will allow a process to go deeper.

## Develop and Support Leadership

*Leadership is the intentional and skillful use of power (which is neutral but always functioning) in order to affect what matters to us.*

— Rev. angel Kyodo Williams

I've seen time and again the centrality of leadership to the success of transformational processes and all organizational health. Activities like planning, culture change, anti-oppression efforts, and team development require vision and courage. Holding out a compelling case for why change is needed and what it might look like requires leadership, and leadership is required to sustain commitment and stick with efforts when things get tough.

There are many different styles and ways of being a leader. Leadership is an expression of power that can be applied to oppress or to liberate. It can be formally conferred based on position and role or informal and situationally exercised. Ideally, when leadership is held as Power With, it lives in all roles and with all people in an organization. Organizational dysfunction can happen when leadership is misapplied, misused, or limited to those in top positions.

I think of leadership that liberates as a shining light that provides direction, illuminates possibility, and holds a flame for others to ignite and thrive in their own leadership. As I understand leadership, it is a way of being, not a set of tasks. I believe leadership for liberation comes from a deep place inside ourselves that we reach by understanding ourselves, our motivations, our identities, and our impact on others.

We often hear that children pay more attention to what their parents and guardians do than what they say. So it is with organizational leadership. The behavior of leaders, particularly those with positional responsibility, sets the tone. Leaders influence culture and most of what happens inside organizations, even when we don't trust or respect them. I believe the adage that the personal limits of leaders become the limits of the organization.

*"I really want everyone here to have a good work/life balance,"* Molly, *the executive director of a small non-profit, told me, "But often*

*folks are here late into the evening and are coming in on weekends. I
just can't get them to stop."*

*"What time do you leave?" I asked.*

*"Usually around 9 pm," Molly offered, "but I'm the ED... I need
to do that."*

In my experience, if top leaders are not on board, change
efforts will eventually stall. Top leaders have the institutional
power to initiate, sustain, or stop activities and distribution
of resources. Their behavior, actions, and attitudes can either
model or undermine the vulnerability and commitment needed
for change to take root. Pressure from the bottom up can help
catalyze change, but if the gatekeepers aren't on board, it will
be very, very difficult to sustain.

I believe that supporting the growth and development of
people in positional leadership roles is a key lever in any change
initiative. They need thinking partnership, support, and spaces
to lean into their own transformation — even when they have
great capacity and have already done an enormous amount of
personal work.

If our goal is to support leadership everywhere in the system,
we must address the question of which people to involve, how,
and when. It can be easy to focus an intervention on people at
a single level of the organization: front line workers, middle
managers, top executives. However, I believe that for an entire
system to move, people throughout the organization must be
intimately involved. So how do we target and sequence our
intervention?

I have found that, like so much else in organizational
development consulting, it completely depends on the goals of
the initiative and the condition of the system. On the one hand,
we want to break down barriers that have kept many from
accessing power because we want our interventions to create

more just workplaces and shared power. On the other hand, if we move too far ahead of the positional leaders, the work itself may not take root or be sustained.

Leadership development and support can include:

- 1:1 coaching to support behavior change, emotional needs, and skill development. This often includes building awareness of personal motivations, sharing tools to access internal strengths and resources, clarifying vision, and supporting leaders to lean into appropriate vulnerability.
- External perspectives. The familiar refrain that it's lonely at the top is in fact a reality. It can feel risky for staff to speak truth to power, which can leave top leaders unaware of critical perspectives. Coaches and consultants can provide a much needed outside perspective and support leaders to pull back from the day-to-day and take a wider view of their landscape.
- Thinking partnership for problem solving. Leaders need a trusted place of vulnerability where they can try on ideas.
- Training and other learning opportunities to build skills and capacity (e.g., facilitation skills, coaching, supervision).
- Opportunities for solidarity and connection with other leaders such as peer coaching and Communities of Practice (small groups of people who meet regularly to learn together about a particular topic).

It's an honor to work with leaders who have the courage to look inside themselves to ground their work in a deeper place of knowing and being. I've been asked why we need to attend to our inner condition when there is so much suffering in the world. Why spend time and energy on ourselves when others are starving? Isn't it wrong to take time away from the vital work at hand?

It's been my experience that when we don't attend to our internal condition, we continue to perpetuate harm. As Richard Rohr teaches, "That which doesn't get transformed gets transmitted." This is particularly relevant for those of us who have been socialized into dominance. When we do not work to heal our wounds, hurts, and mistaken facticity, they leak out and onto other people in harmful ways. Years ago, as we were engaged in a conversation about racism and whiteness, my colleague, Kristen Handricken, and my then young daughter, Zoe Grodsky, collaboratively coined the term "oprivious" to represent the phenomenon of continuing to perpetuate oppression because we are oblivious to our privilege.

Margo, a white woman, was Vice President of BTB, an ethical clothing company with 50 employees. She had been with the company for over 20 years during which she had risen from purchaser to VP.

Despite BTB's commitment to environmentally-friendly products and fair-trading practices, they had thought very little about racial justice and systemic oppression within their organization or in their business and sourcing practices. Margo knew that in order to truly realize their mission of fair equitable trade between the global North and global South, BTB needed to commit to addressing these issues.

Out of 7 team members on the senior leadership team, there was one other white woman, one man of South Asian heritage, and four white men. All were cis-gender, and only one team member publicly identified as queer. Teams throughout the company had a pattern of white men at the top and women and Black, Indigenous, and other people of color in the lower-level jobs.

Margo contacted my colleague and me, a cross-race consulting team, for help. As we listened to her, we learned that she had the positional and persuasive power to initiate the process of creating a racial justice commitment inside of BTB, but her fear was holding her back. It was a radical thing to do within the company, and she was worried about backlash — against the company, against any further engagement in this work, and against her. Scared of the possible consequences, she had disavowed her power to initiate and lead anti-racism efforts.

For the project to succeed, Margo needed to own her power and courageously provide strong leadership.

We started with intensive leadership coaching to help her connect to her vision, courage, will, and fortitude. We helped her see her pattern of disavowing power and its cost to her and the organization. Pretending that she did not have power meant that nothing was happening, and BTB continued to undermine, underutilize, and underpay women and Black, Indigenous, and other people of color.

We used the Immunity to Change process (see Tools and Resources) for this work, and Margo had a breakthrough when she understood how she had been socialized as a white woman to internalize sexism. With our ongoing support, she moved more fully into the required leadership. While she was still scared, she was also resolute and clear. She no longer wanted to stand in her own way.

When she broached the subject with the CEO, Frank, Margo was surprised to discover that he agreed with her and was ready to begin. While he didn't fully understand the effort, he supported it and Margo's leadership both publicly and privately.

We supported Margo in creating a diverse planning team to partner with her to guide BTB's anti-racism and anti-oppression efforts. The committee was advisory to her, and she and Frank were the final decision-makers.

As we worked with Margo to build a shared commitment to the initiative among the planning team, we put a lot of attention into relationships and trust-building right from the start. Over several meetings, they shared stories about themselves and their identities. We created space for them to talk honestly about how racism and oppression were present at BTB in general and for them personally. We built a shared framework and vocabulary for understanding and discussing systemic oppression.

Over time, the planning team took on increasing investment and responsibility for the initiative's success, rolling out extensive learning programs and policy and practice reviews throughout the organization. Margo needed to stand fully in her power, leadership, and vision as she practiced Power With with the team.

The process was iterative — the more she stood firmly and clearly in her power and leadership and supported the leadership of others, the more trust, care, and responsibility others took on for the work, and the better able she was to continue to bring Frank along. The more others joined with her, the stronger her resolve — and the initiative — became.

As I wrote in my earlier work, *Where Does It Hurt: Health and Disharmony in Organizational Ecosystems*, leadership growth "is life-long work requiring both humility and courage: the humility to know that we are always a work in progress, that we never arrive at a place of perfection where we are done with our inner work." Organizational transformation for justice requires leaders who are willing to engage in this deeply personal work, continually re-orient themselves toward love, and shine their light brightly.

## Tell The Truth

*The heart of justice is truth telling, seeing ourselves and the world the way it is rather than the way we want it to be.*

— bell hooks

*Not everything that is faced can be changed, but nothing can be changed until it is faced.*

— James Baldwin

When I was first learning to consult, my mentor, Kate Howell, offered a workshop on organizational development. She told a story about skillfully managing a very complex situation.

"How did you know how to do that?" someone asked, awestruck.

"I learned how to tell the truth," Kate humbly replied.

Truth held with compassion creates space to sit in the legacy of the past, the discomfort of the present, and the uncertainty of the future. From this place of alignment, transformation is possible. When a group of people can move together from a place of shared truth, it is like rocket fuel.

This begs the obvious question, "What is truth?" Philosophers through the ages have struggled with this question. I have spent much of my adult life learning how to locate and speak my truth, knowing it is only a partial piece of a larger picture filtered through my lenses of identity and experience. We all have our own truths. But I am talking here about organizational truth: the truth of peoples' experiences within the organization; the truth of the larger context in which the organization is situated; the truth of the impact of the organization's work, the behaviors of its people, and the mental models and unspoken assumptions it holds. When we don't see or speak a fuller truth, we can develop misguided and even destructive strategies.

Truth is essential for healing, growth, and justice, but speaking it can feel risky, even dangerous. On the other hand, unspoken truths can be like a pebble in a shoe — easy to ignore at first, but catalysts for gaping wounds when left unaddressed.

I frequently hear people in meetings start comments by saying "I'm sorry to be such a bummer" or speak with cheerful countenances that barely mask the untold wells of pain beneath. I believe both these stances reflect the idea that what may be hard to hear should not be spoken.

Yet over and over, I have seen that not speaking truth significantly reduces organizational effectiveness. I can think of dozens of examples where skirting around truth and failing to address issues at hand escalated over months and years into full-blown organizational crisis and negative impacts on individual health and well-being.

The impact of privilege allows some to comfortably avoid seeing truth and forces others to exhaust themselves as they work to accommodate the denial of what is obvious to them. Part of what keeps white dominance in place is the conditioning white people have around avoiding pain at all costs — especially the pain of really feeling the impact of racism and the enduring suffering from the legacy of slavery and genocide in the founding of the US. White supremacy teaches white people that we are entitled to comfort. That we should not see the truth, speak the truth, or rock the boat. As a result, we numb ourselves and deliberately cut ourselves off from our own inner resources so we don't have to face uncomfortable truths.

The risks of knowing and speaking truths in unsafe environments can be very real. Being the person who calls out "The emperor has no clothes!" like the child in the Hans Christian Andersen tale can bring the possibility of reward or punishment. How will you be received? Will there be reprisal?

Racism and other oppressions can make truth-telling truly dangerous. People can dismiss and undermine the credibility of truth-tellers. This can get particularly dangerous when people employ racist and other stereotypes (e.g., "angry Black woman").

Outsiders can play a critical role in helping the truth come out safely. Barry Oshry called facilitators "designated listeners." I see consultants as designated truth-tellers, courting and beckoning forth deeper truths. We are often in a position to say what feels unsayable to folks on the inside.

What truths can we tell as consultants? How do we know when it is time to tell a truth? We don't walk in the door and blurt out, "Man, is it ever stinky in here!" If we want truth to be accepted and acted upon, we need to surface the right truth with the right people in the right way. Anne Lamott writes, "you don't always have to chop with the sword of truth, you can point with it too."

I seek to surface and, when it is appropriate for me to do so, name previously unacknowledged truths. When I discern that a strategy is ineffective, a leader is not providing appropriate guidance, whole communities are not being considered in resource allocation, or a colleague's behavior is demeaning and harmful, I talk with people to confirm my understanding and ask what is keeping them from speaking what they know to be true. They may perceive danger in speaking these things aloud, citing examples of reprisal to justify their fear. But often they just didn't think they could until they realized differently during our conversation.

When I want to name a truth I think I see, I usually frame my observations as hypotheses, with curiosity. "Might it be true that...?" "I am seeing x. Is that true?" The point is not to be right or put forth the most insightful analysis. The goal is to bring out the truths that are present so others can see the situation more clearly. I have witnessed tears of relief and gratitude when people finally speak their truths and their colleagues receive them as valid.

I have learned so much from witnessing my colleague, Joyce Shabazz, lead hundreds of people through transformational processes of confronting truths and, over time, rewiring their hearts and minds. Joyce is a highly skilled and experienced educator and facilitator with a crystal-clear anti-oppression analysis. But there is something else she does that makes transformation possible. She holds people and herself steadfastly with dignity. She never loses sight of our shared humanity, and she is kind and compassionate as she clearly speaks her truth and helps others to see the truth of their systems.

Truth alone is not a magic wand. It needs to be heard, met seriously, and followed by action. But as Rabbi Danya Ruttenberg has said, "If we can get the truth telling done right, real truth telling, the next step will present itself."

On a crisp fall day, I took a long walk with Ted, a retired executive director and former client. As we strolled along the Charles River catching up on our lives, he reminded me of a powerful experience of truth from years earlier, when I facilitated some visioning and planning with his organization.

"We were scared to 'come out' as an organization — to let people know who we really were," he told me. "We were afraid that people would see us as too radical. We imagined we would drive funders away if we talked about what we believed and actually did. After you encouraged us to do that, things changed. It was absolutely the opposite of what we feared. Most people responded with so much enthusiasm. Maybe we lost a few people, but we gained so many more. We clarified our base, and our funding became stable for the first time."

Commitment to justice compels us to speak and welcome truth. When Ted's organization shared the fullness of who they were and what they believed, they transformed their relationship with stakeholders and funders and brought their work to a new level. These kinds of results are not guaranteed, and the risks need to be taken mindfully so that our actions and words bring us closer, and not further, from our goals.

## Practice Accountability

*You don't rise to the level of your goals. You fall to the level of your systems.*

— James Cleary

*We need to erect structures that curb our worst instincts and endorse and give incentives to our better angels.*

—Ta-Nehisi Coates

Accountability is essential for organizational effectiveness, but it's a place where many justice-oriented people and organizations struggle. Most of us have been swimming our whole lives in a punitive and dehumanizing framework of accountability that has turned us off the whole concept. We need to reimagine ways of holding ourselves, each other, and our organizations accountable that are grounded in our commitment to transformation, love, and justice. When we go off course, like the humans we are, we need to develop ways to bring ourselves back with dignity, compassion, and rigor. Creating accountability with love is part of the work of our times, as we figure out what it really looks like to operate justly outside of dominance and subjugation.

When we are accountable, we fulfill our commitments and responsibilities. We work to align the impact of our behaviors and actions with our values and aspirations. Just accountability is rooted in being able to locate, speak, and absorb the truth of when we are in alignment and when we are not.

Organizational assessments can often reveal accountability issues, particularly if we specifically ask about things like follow-through, meeting goals, and ways of being and behaving. Often, though, the absence of accountability emerges over time as engagements progress and the roots of disharmonies become clearer.

Some of the symptoms that a system lacks accountability include:

- Failure to meet organizational and individual goals
- Areas of work falling through cracks
- Duplication of work
- Difficult and harmful behaviors
- Interpersonal tensions
- Stagnant and ineffective staff
- Ineffective leadership
- Ineffective governance
- General dissatisfaction
- Staff overwork and burnout
- High rates of staff attrition

Here are some of the issues that can underlie lack of accountability:

- Mental models that erroneously hold love and accountability as mutually exclusive
- Conflating accountability with punishment and constraint
- Fear that accountability will limit creativity and autonomy
- Fear that if we're held accountable, we won't measure up
- Fear of losing relationships
- Fear of being negatively judged if people are made uncomfortable or feel badly in our presence
- Fear of being oppressive
- Fear of risk to job security and livelihood
- The mindfucks of racism and systemic oppression, which can confuse and cloud accountability (along with everything else they touch). White people can experience guilt and shame when they need to hold a Black, Indigenous, or other person of color accountable. Black, Indigenous, and other people of color can sometimes feel unsafe and worry about backlash if they need to hold their colleagues accountable
- The tension between support and accountability, which are chronically out of balance in capitalist culture; an outsized emphasis on compliance and fear-based motivation frames needing support as weakness

I believe that just accountability is multi-directional across levels of power rather than a top-down proposition. It means holding each other as humans, with dignity, while also holding clear boundaries, expectations, and commitments to outcomes. Accountability can be intrinsically motivated, structurally dictated, or fostered by culture, context, and relationship.

My wise friend and HR expert, Maxine Hart, says that, "Accountability has become too big an idea. It's overloaded and feels enormous and vague. We need to break it down. Specifically, what are we agreeing to?"

Here are some specific areas where consultants can help organizations move toward greater accountability grounded in justice:

- *Norms and Expectations*
  Norms and expectations are integral to creating just organizational cultures. Unstated expectations and norms privilege those who know the codes of dominance. Articulating shared norms across cultures and identities can be a liberating and challenging experience. When we codify and agree to expectations, we have a basis for surfacing and addressing difficult and harmful behaviors.

  Organizations and teams can collaboratively develop explicit agreements about expected behaviors, communication, and ways of working, and clearly articulate behaviors that are not acceptable (e.g., sexual harassment, racist remarks) and their consequences. When new staff come on board, supervisors and colleagues need to make sure that they understand and are aligned with existing agreements.

  Norms and expectations should always be open for discussion and interrogation. Seemingly good ideas that don't take into account specific individual or group needs, like accessibility or cultural practices, can have unintended consequences that need to be addressed.

  Articulating and agreeing on norms and expectations both requires and builds trust.

- *Outcome-Oriented Goals*

  For organizations to be effective, we need to know clearly what we are accountable for achieving and how and when our work will be measured. Without clear goals, people may spend too much time on tasks that don't advance the organization's mission. Individual goals should always align with larger organizational goals and values.

  Goals should be developed collaboratively between the person who will drive them and the supervisors, team members, and other stakeholders who can help ensure they are aligned and achievable. It builds team cohesion when team members understand how each other's work contributes to meeting collective goals.

  Systems that support people in achieving goals include:
  - realistic timelines and appropriate resources
  - ongoing supervision and support to address challenges
  - agreed upon measures of success
  - milestones for evaluation and reflection
- *Clear Roles and Responsibilities*

  People need to know what their jobs are and what they are responsible for, plain and simple. Lack of clarity about structures and roles is confusing and creates a vacuum for power to be misapplied.

  Unclear structures can lead to too many cooks in the kitchen and people stepping over — or even trampling — each other as they try to fill in gaps. Important tasks and outcomes can go untended. Conflict that appears as interpersonal tension may in fact result from lack of structure.

  One tool for clarifying roles and responsibilities is a Decision Matrix, which lays out roles, responsibilities, and commitments for different areas of work and decision-making (see Tools and Resources). Everyone in the organization needs a clear job description that they and their colleagues understand. All members of a team should understand each other's roles and how the team will accomplish its responsibilities.

- *Feedback*

  Robert Gass talks about "feedback rich organizations." Feedback is an ongoing investment in growth and development so that people have the skill and capacity they need to carry out their roles — not a thing that happens only when something goes wrong.

  Rather than a one-way street, feedback is ideally a dialogue in which everyone involved is curious to investigate what they need and can learn to do their jobs well.

  A culture of loving feedback and authentic dialogue requires people to build skills for authentic dialogue and institutionalizing structures for feedback and non-punitive reviews (e.g., peer reviews, employee evaluations). These structures should include support for staff growth and development, and plans for addressing challenging areas. It is also important to have clear measures and a shared understanding of what happens when goals are not met or actions and behaviors don't align with the organization's norms and expectations.

- *Processes to Address Harm*

  Letting difficult behaviors and harm go unaddressed or dealing with them only in punitive ways (e.g., termination, loss of responsibilities) engenders further harm, conflict, negative health impacts, and disenfranchisement.

  It is possible to build a culture of accountability around harm. Organizations can normalize addressing difficult behaviors through honest conversation, formal and informal evaluation and feedback, and institutionalized restorative practices (e.g., circle processes) that acknowledge the impact of harm and identify means of repair. Through these processes, it is possible for people to understand the impact of their behaviors and take responsibility changing behaviors and remediating the effects of their actions. Cultures of accountability create contexts for people to continually grow more trustworthy and compassionate.

There may be situations that cannot be resolved in ways that lead to restoration of relationships and trust, and sometimes people cannot continue to work in the organization. But what differentiates just processes is that we never lose sight of the humanity and dignity of all the individuals involved.

When enacted with care — and intentional attention to these elements — accountability helps maximize individual and community well-being and organizational effectiveness.

## Clarify Guiding Ideas

*Walk with purpose, collide with destiny.*

— Bertice Berry

When my daughter Sasha was in sixth grade, she taught me what makes objects magnetic: all the electrons in an item rotate in the same direction. When electrons are spinning in different directions, there is no magnetic power; when they are aligned, magnetism and power! So it is with people in organizations.

"Guiding Ideas," a term I learned from fellow consultant Jay Vogt, are the constellation of ideas that umbrella an organization's work, typically its mission, vision, and values. I sometimes hear them referred to as "North Stars," the consistent and dependable elements that guide the organization's direction.

Guiding Ideas reflect our aspirations; they expand our imagination of what's possible and help us see our desired future as attainable. They provide guidance and context for all that happens in an organization and are one of the most important things an organization should have. In addition to being integral to strategic thinking, planning, and action, Guiding Ideas are the foundation of mission- and values-driven branding.

The process of articulating Guiding Ideas can reveal the previously unspoken assumptions and mental models that are driving the behavior and actions of individuals as well as the organization's strategy, goals, activities, and use of resources. When an organization has not articulated or communicated its Guiding Ideas, people fill in the holes for themselves and operate under their individual understandings. Unarticulated or competing Guiding Ideas are a source of much organizational disharmony.

Inclusive processes to clarify Guiding Ideas are usually energizing for organizations and fun and inspiring for me. These processes need to create space for listening, truth-telling, and generative conflict. Their goal is not just to put words on paper but to collectively and accurately represent the organization's longings and aspirations. Explicating Guiding Ideas and the assumptions underlying them can surface ideological conflicts that are often bubbling just under the surface. This opening invites a call for honest dialogue.

Sometimes Guiding Ideas and rigorous annual planning are all an organization needs for clarity and direction; a strategic plan becomes unnecessary. When people in an organization have a shared sense of what they stand for, where they are heading, and why, they can see how their daily work contributes to something larger than themselves. In other words, like those magnets, they align, spin in the same direction, and produce power!

Here is how I define each of the elements of Guiding Ideas:

- *Mission* conveys an organization's purpose (why it exists and what it is here to do) and defines the work it does to fulfill its purpose. I like missions that give a concise taste of an organization's special sauce, ideally in one or two brief sentences.

  As statements, missions are both internal (e.g., used by the staff and board) and external (e.g., used in materials and communications for the public). Everyone in an organization should know and understand the mission.

  Missions are current — they are what we are here to do NOW.

  Here's an example of a mission statement from my client organization the Center for Restorative Programs (CRP): *Strengthen community in the San Luis Valley by building connection, transforming conflict, and healing relationships.*

- A *Vision* is a statement of desired impact, that is, a picture of the successful future our work will bring about. A vision can be long term, perhaps not even in our lifetime (e.g., eliminating hunger), or situated in a closer time frame that we can imagine but do not yet occupy. A vision can provide an organization with inspiring and unifying focus.

  Visions are the future — where we want to be.

  Here is CRP's vision: *Restorative Practices are the foundation of a healthy and just community throughout the San Luis Valley.*

- *Values* are what the organization stands for. They are the beliefs that the organization puts into action.

  Values are aspirational and guide us in the present. They are what we believe in, not necessarily what we live perfectly right now. They shape our actions in the current moment even as we strive to align those actions with our aspirations. Here are CRP's Values (Please note that "justness" is not a typo, it's a word that they coined themselves):

*Relationship*
*We all have a need for healthy connections and relationships with others. All people deserve the opportunity to build healthy relationships rooted in deep understanding.*

*Community*
*Community is built on complex and interdependent relationships, including interpersonal, organizational, and systemic. A healthy community requires mutual understanding and respect rooted in deep listening and authentic communication.*

*Meaningful Accountability*
*Our words and actions have ripples of impact. True accountability is possible when we own the impact of our words and actions; when we take responsibility for our own behaviors and allow others to take responsibility for theirs; and when we strive to repair harms as meaningfully as possible.*

*Equity and Justness*
*We currently live in a society where systemic obstacles in the justice system, education, and access to resources often negatively impact marginalized groups. Preventing and repairing harm in individual relationships and within systems helps interrupt racism, misogyny, homophobia, and other forms of oppression, allowing everyone to have greater access to achieving their full potential.*

*Empowerment*
*We all have the right to transform our lives and heal from the impact of harm we have caused or experienced. When we have*

*agency to act and speak on our own behalf, we grow stronger and more resilient.*

*Dignity*
*Every person has dignity and value. Our community is stronger when each person has an opportunity to be heard and respected, particularly those that have been historically marginalized.*

Common Life, a grassroots community development organization in a relatively small city, had to decide how to use a piece of land they were caretaking. Unused for the five years it had been under their control, the land had become a dumping ground for trash and created a sizable rat problem. If they didn't figure out a good use for the land within the next year, Common Life would permanently lose it.

Board and staff members had many different ideas about what to do, including letting the land go. While there was some urgency to make a decision, it was unclear how the land fitted into the organization's bigger picture. The situation had surfaced other underlying organizational disharmonies as well. There was no shared clarity about Common Life's purpose or priorities and no clear understanding of roles or decision-making processes — including how to make the decision about the land.

The relatively new ED, Arya, the staff, and the board were all confused, stuck, and frustrated. At the urging of a staff member, Arya called me.

It was unclear how to begin, so I contracted to do an assessment to get a clearer picture of what was happening. I interviewed several board and staff members and learned that they were committed, idealistic, hardworking, caring people. I also saw that confusion, grumbling, wasted time, and mistrust consumed a great deal of organizational and human energy.

I recommended they form a planning committee of a few board members and an equal number of staff members, including Arya, to work with me. After some activities to warm up and build group agreements, the planning committee developed a proposal for an inclusive process to define the organization's Guiding Ideas: we would hold a board and staff retreat for broad input, the committee would create a draft, Arya would approve the draft, and the board would have final approval. We also proposed that they then form a second committee to make a recommendation for the best strategic use of the land on the basis of the completed Guiding Ideas.

Arya strongly supported this proposal, and the board approved it and communicated the process to the staff.

We held a one and a half-day retreat with the board and staff to identify a clear purpose for the organization, articulate organizational values, and develop a shared vision of the future. By moving together slowly and carefully, we created a container for deep listening. We were able to build trust and achieve all our desired outcomes.

The Guiding Ideas that emerged from the process centered around creating community food security in poor neighborhoods, a need created by historical and ongoing oppression. Once the Guiding Ideas were clear, it was relatively easy to determine a solution for the land. They decided to use it to start an incubator for immigrant and refugee farmers. This economic empowerment project supported people recently arrived in the US, promoted food security in their community, fostered sustainable farming practices, and built community around growing food.

Loss is a natural part of the process of achieving the focus Common Life sought. Two board members were unhappy with both the Guiding Ideas and the decision about the land. They wanted a public park with pop-up commerce and did not share the emerging commitment to supporting economically under-resourced communities. They advocated for their plans, but the rest of the board and staff were clear. The two board members left the organization.

Common Life used its Guiding Ideas as the basis for multiple three-year strategic and annual operating plans. I had the great joy of seeing them achieve a lot of success as I worked with them on and off until Arya retired more than ten years later — all of it grounded in their carefully crafted Guiding Ideas.

If an organization is going to articulate its Guiding Ideas, particularly its values, it must be willing to tell the truth about its current lived reality. It's beautiful to say that equity and justice are core values. However, making that statement without demonstrated commitment to addressing practices, policies, behaviors, and culture that may be furthering inequity is hypocritical, exhausting, demoralizing, and undermining.

I encourage my clients to make their Guiding Ideas part of their everyday lives, keeping them front and center in all aspects of their work and culture. "How does this align with our mission, vision, and values?" should become an automatic question for discernment.

It's essential to continually align Guiding Ideas with the organization's lived reality, including strategy, structure, and culture. When held with care, this alignment can foster powerful movement toward being the change the organization is trying to create in the world.

## Imagine and Plan for the Future

*We often tell our students, "the future is in your hands." But I think the future is actually in your mouth. You have to articulate the world you want to live in first.*

— Ocean Vuong

To create the world as we want it to be, we need visions of compelling future possibilities and plans that help us apply our energy and resources to get there.

I sometimes start planning processes by asking people to share the first words that come to mind when they hear the word *planning*. Confining. Exciting. Rigid. Clarity. A Waste of Time. Essential. In most groups, the words are all over the map, representing many different experiences and attitudes.

Solid planning creates alignment and clarity. I think of it like a laser beam. When our energy is focused and aligned, we have power. When we are unfocused, our energy, like light, is scattered, and our power dissipates. Plans guide how we apply our resources. They give us energy to live into our purpose and provide measures against which we can test new ideas. They keep us moving toward where we want to be.

A plan can also be a vehicle for innovation and a landing strip for creativity. Innovation and transformational solutions emerge over time as we listen carefully to the world around us and learn new ideas and ways of being. Without plans, we can lack clarity, direction, and forward momentum; without flexibility and space for learning and emergence, we can find ourselves lulled into a false sense of certainty and locked into trajectories that may not serve our interests.

At the same time, planning and plans can be held too rigidly. They can create guardrails that stifle creativity and don't allow for learning, exploration, and experimentation. Good plans provide the context and shape within which creativity can thrive, and good planning processes offer a chance to dream and learn.

I've facilitated hundreds of planning processes, from year-long strategic planning to project planning, event planning, annual planning, and more. There is no one-size-fits-all type of plan, and no two processes are quite the same.

Different types of planning meet different kinds of needs. Planning is sometimes categorized into strategic and operational/tactical. In reality, the two are iterative. Operational plans need to be grounded in strategic thinking, and strategic plans need to be manifested with operational plans. Still, I find the distinction helpful as I design Process Maps to guide planning processes.

Operational or tactical planning is grounded in the short term. Its parameters are the strategic directions we have already set. Then we need a plan to accomplish what we're going to do in alignment with our Guiding Ideas. For example, we are running a summer program for youth to learn carpentry. How do we best hire and train staff? How will we recruit young people? Etc.

Strategic planning is more comprehensive. It has a longer time horizon and asks fundamental questions about who we are and what we're here to accomplish. We take stock of who we are, what we believe, and what's happening around us to paint a picture of the result we want to achieve and how we will apply our resources to get there. We often start with revisiting or defining our Guiding Ideas and undertaking a SWOT analysis, which looks at the internal organization (strengths and weaknesses) and external landscape (opportunities and threats). Only then do we turn to creating future plans.

In strategic planning, we need to create the trust for folks to step away from their current constraints to dream and a process that helps them come back to the ground to design realistic pathways for implementation.

Reasons to embark on strategic planning can include:

- Lack of clarity about who the organization is and what it stands for
- Lack of organizational focus and direction
- Significant changes in the external environment that the organization must figure out how to navigate
- Lack of clarity about what the organization needs to do to travel toward their desired future
- New leadership with a new vision
- Need for a new vision

There are many different ways to do strategic planning, and the amount of time needed varies widely. At one end, I've facilitated groups to complete a simple strategic plan in two days. At the other, I am currently in the middle of two processes where complex organizations are taking over a year to do the work at a slow, deliberate, and non-taxing pace.

As with everything I do, I'm always looking to match the purpose and desired outcomes of planning with the appropriate process to create clarity and alignment for the organization in all its uniqueness. I work with my clients to design processes that will allow them to move with grace and curiosity at a pace that works for them and adjust as needed once we get going.

Questions that help us shape the plan and process include:

- Why is this plan needed?
- What questions should this plan answer?
- How clear are the "Guiding Ideas" that will inform the plan?

- What is the time horizon of the plan (e.g., a five-year strategic plan vs. an operational plan for the next six months)?
  - How stable or fixed are the internal and external environments? Are there likely to be significant changes inside the organization, the sector, or the world that might impact the time horizon? We don't want to build a plan that we know could quickly become obsolete.
- How will the plan be used?
  - How nimble do we want this plan to be?
  - What's the style of the primary leader(s) who will be accountable to ensuring the plan's success? How much detail do they need to implement the plan well (e.g., entrepreneurial with big ideas vs. detailed and logistical)?
- What are the planning parameters?
  - What kinds of resources and time are available for planning?
  - Who should be involved in planning and in what capacity? What will make the planning as inclusive as practically possible? Whose voices are critical? How will decisions be made?
  - What do we already know about constraints and givens (e.g., funding constraints that dictate mandatory programs)?
  - Are there other relevant processes happening that could impact or synergize with planning (e.g., branding)?

Interaction Institute for Social Change's strategic framework of *Where are we now? Where do we want to be?* and *How do we get there?* is an incredibly useful guide for process design (see Tools and Resources).

- **Where Are We Now?**
  - ○ What is true in our internal and external landscape that we need to pay attention to?
  - ○ What is our purpose (and/or mission and values)? Why are we here?
  - ○ What assumptions and beliefs do we currently hold about our work?
- **Where Do We Want to Be?**
  - ○ What are our vision and goals? When we are successful, what will it look like?
- **How Will We Get There?**
  - ○ What actions will we take?
  - ○ What resources and capacities will we need?
  - ○ Roles and Responsibilities (**Who** will do **What** by **When?**).

Dream It Together had been through a series of leadership transitions, one consequence of which was significant mission drift. The values of this community-based organization were clear, but their programs were all over the map. As a result, program quality was variable, their resources were spread thin, and their staff were exhausted.

When two staff members, Tariq and Monica, took over as co-executive directors, I worked with them to clarify their priorities and directions. We formed a planning committee of program participants, board members, staff, and community members. We spent time up front building relationships and trust among the committee. The committee and I conducted interviews and surveys and facilitated gatherings to gain input from all stakeholders (staff, board, program participants, allies, and funders) about their hopes and dreams for Dream

It Together. This approach to engagement built further cohesion and trust within the organization and with program participants.

The committee synthesized what they had gathered from their wider community and used the organization's values to help identify a clear purpose, goals, and specific pathways for achieving those goals. Dream It Together had several major unknowns, including future funding and a possible move, so we developed strategy filters and benchmarks for success that had a significant degree of flexibility.

Tariq and Monica made the strategic plan a daily presence in their work, talking about it frequently, using it to make decisions, organizing board and staff work around strategic goals, and deliberately moving forward on its path. Over 15 years later, Dream It Together is thriving, and members of the planning committee still talk about this process as an important and seminal moment, organizationally and personally.

Organizations often call with requests for strategic planning, but once we start talking, many discover it's not actually what they need. It's important to assess how ready organizations are for planning and whether planning is the right intervention for the questions they are asking. To assess readiness, I ask about:

- The choice to plan now
- The current level of clarity, alignment, or divergence around the issues central to planning
- Their capacity to sustain the kind of process their questions will require

- The level of trust within the system
- What else is going on in the organization that could impact the planning process or their work overall

If the answers to these questions reveal a lack of capacity, widespread disagreement or mistrust, or an absence of strategic questions, they may need other processes before they undertake planning.

---

Nora, the board chair of a small, overwhelmingly white healthcare organization set up a time to talk with me. She wanted to see if I might be available to help them with strategic planning. When we spoke, I asked my usual questions, listening for what they wanted to do and why.

"Why now?" I asked her.

"Well, we have a calendar. Every five years we do a plan, and we're in year four, so it's time," she replied.

To help assess what kind of process might be useful at this time, I asked, "What are your big questions? What don't you know about who you are, where you're going, and what you do?"

Nora replied, "We don't really have any big questions. We're pretty clear about what we're doing and why. Things are going well. One interesting thing," she went on, "is that we've hired a Diversity, Equity, and Inclusion consultant to do an assessment."

"Oh, what did you learn from that?" I asked, eager to hear.

"It's still in process. She'll work with a committee of board and staff to put together a report, but it's going to take a while." There was not yet a plan for what they would do with the assessment once they received it.

"Tell me about the level of awareness and commitment to anti-racism, equity, and inclusion within the organization," I requested.

"I'm sorry to say that it's very low for most people," she replied timidly. "Most people haven't thought much about it at all."

"How did it happen that you agreed to engage a consultant and do this assessment?" I asked.

Nora explained that she, the executive director, and one other board member had proposed it, and the rest agreed. I had seen this before: predominantly white organizations agreeing to engage in diversity work without understanding what it would entail and that they would be required to examine and change many things.

I learned in our conversation that they had limited time and resources for processes. A strategic planning process would likely take up much of that energy. I thought about sequencing and how an organization-wide understanding of racism and dominance should ideally inform a planning process. "I'm imagining that the assessment will tell you a lot," I said. "Completing and understanding the assessment will likely shift your understanding of who you are and your ideas of who you want to be. You will hopefully learn a lot about how whiteness and other forms of dominance are showing up and driving you. I think it will serve you best to understand and metabolize that before putting time and energy into developing a new plan."

A big light bulb went off for Nora. She quickly saw that this was true.

At that moment, this organization and I were not a fit for each other. They had an important path to walk, and they had already taken some essential steps down it. It could be easy for them to see the assessment, say thank you very much, and do nothing with it. They would likely have hired me to do strategic planning, but I believe it would have been a distraction from the opportunity before them. Perhaps in the future, we will work together when the timing is right.

## A Story of Transformational Change

"The Group," an overwhelmingly white and relatively small national professional association, engaged me nearly 20 years ago to help them pull their organization out of a difficult time. Many feared the organization would implode in on itself. It seemed like a very real possibility to me.

The board was entirely elected by the membership. They had just hired their first-ever paid staff person, Callie, a younger white woman, to be their first ED. Before Callie's hire, The Group was managed and run entirely by its volunteer board.

Callie was bright, eager, and inexperienced; her knowledge of membership organizations was minimal. The board's decision to hire an ED had caused an uproar among the members, many of whom feared losing control of the organization. Trust was frayed, and politicking was rampant. Angry members called board members at home, and letters with doomsday scenarios circulated on the membership listserv.

I interviewed Callie and each board member before we gathered for an in-person retreat at a small college in the US Midwest. It was clear from my interviews that the conflict was between the board and a significant faction of the membership and within the membership itself.

Within the board, there was a high degree of trust in each other and Callie. To her great credit, Callie knew that the conflict swirling within the organization was not about her, though several members had publicly said unkind and condescending things about her.

Though it was long ago, I will never forget the fear and anxiety board members brought into the room at our first retreat. Lines of worry and concern were visible on several of their faces. After we settled into the meeting, clarified our POP, and had a chance to check in, I asked everyone to speak to their current thoughts about the tension within the organization in a circle listening process (see Tools and Resources). The board and Callie agreed that she would be part of this process.

"They just don't see that we needed to do this," Larry, the board chair, said. "They don't understand how much we were doing. We have full-time jobs. We were burning out."

Susan, the Vice Chair, noted, "Members aren't just worried about the professionalization of the staff."

Long-term board member Janet added, "What's worrying them is what this association stands for and what we'll do in the future."

Many heads nodded in agreement.

The board recognized that they had greatly underestimated the impact of hiring an ED and the upset about the organization's direction it had sparked among members. They had skipped an adaptive process for the highly engaged members of an association that valued democracy and voice to move together into this new phase. "We have to do something fast, or we won't be able to go on as an association," Eddy, a board member, noted.

At the retreat, the board and Callie agreed that they wanted to do whatever they could to restore trust with the membership and set a course for the future based on what the membership wanted. They also affirmed that the move to hire an ED was necessary and the choice of Callie was a good one. They stood by the decision and agreed not to reverse it even though it was within their authority to do so.

I helped them form a steering committee with Callie, three board members, and four organization members who were not on the board. The initial mandate of this committee was to gather a picture of what was going on and what members were asking for. The committee represented people with varying perspectives on the organization and what it should be; there was no majority of any one perspective, and no person represented a perspective alone. Committee members were chosen because of their ability and willingness to work collaboratively with divergent views in a heated situation. My role was to facilitate the committee meetings and help guide the overall process; Callie managed the logistics.

The eight-person committee was spread throughout the US, so it met virtually. Even in the days before Zoom and online collaboration platforms, we were able to establish trust and an excellent working rhythm over the course of several conference calls. The committee shared their views on the situation and built a culture of listening attentively to each other.

Together we did an assessment to gain a shared picture of what was happening within the organization, outside of gossip, fears, and rumors. We wanted to hear from members and outside stakeholders about how they saw the organization's current condition and what hopes and dreams they held for it. The committee, acting with the full empowerment of the board, communicated with members about the process.

Holding "inquiry as intervention" as our frame, we designed an assessment process with three components to build trust and relationships with and among members: a survey for all members; interviews with key members and outside stakeholders by the steering committee and me; and, most importantly, in-person discussion groups and gatherings around the US with Callie and board or committee members, which I helped them to design. Because this was before Zoom, most members had not met Callie virtually or in person.

The primary purpose of all these data-gathering methods was to listen sincerely and respectfully to members. The in-person groups were well attended and well received. Many people were happy to meet Callie and learn that she was highly competent and aligned with the values important to the association.

I facilitated many steering committee meetings for the group to make meaning of the data they gathered. The assessment revealed a substantial lack of clarity and consensus about the organization's purpose and what it was here to do. The committee reached a shared story about the current questions, confusions, and different aspirations members had shared. They better understood how members had experienced Callie's hiring as completely disregarding their voices and concerns. The committee reported all of this to the board.

At the board's direction, the committee and I prepared a day-long session for the annual in-person membership meeting at a retreat center in Atlanta. Larry, the board chair, began the session with an honest and vulnerable statement of where the organization was. Without defensiveness, he spoke about why the board had hired an ED, apologized for their missteps (which the board had already done in writing), and discussed the lack of clarity about the organization's purpose and direction that the assessment had revealed. He concluded by laying out an aspiration to restore trust and listen to the collective wishes of the membership as they planned for the future. Larry's vulnerability and the board's accountability created a critical opening.

At the meeting, committee members and I facilitated small group conversations for members to listen to each other and metabolize the organization's current story which the planning committee had identified. We facilitated meaningful conversations that built the scaffolding to create the organization's Mission, Vision, and Values. After the meeting, the steering committee finalized these Guiding Ideas, and the membership overwhelmingly approved them. We then moved on to an equally inclusive planning process to develop exciting organizational priorities and goals.

The organizational anxiety and indigestion subsided as members listened to each other and built trust. Most members were aligned with the new direction that the organization adopted and were appreciative of the ways it was growing. Under Callie's leadership, The Group successfully implemented their strategic plan. Though some members did leave, a greater number joined.

# 6

# Transformational Change Is Hard Work

*Without inner change, there can be no outer change.*
*Without collective change, no change matters.*
— Rev angel Kyodo Williams

In graduate school I took a class in strategic planning. The professor, Noel McGinn, put us in random groups to do a big project over the course of several weeks, saying "I fully expect that many of you will come to me and beg me to change your group to get you away from 'those people.' But here's the thing — 'those' annoying and hard to work with people are always there. You've got to learn to work with them and the baggage and gifts that they bring. That's as big a piece of the work as anything else you'll do!"

I don't know what else I use from that class almost 30 years later, but I remember this comment all the time! As my husband Jonathan continually reminds me when difficult situations emerge, that is part of the work. Unclear processes, conflict, resistance, discomfort, uncertainty, and the challenges that accompany change are not distractions. They are the signs that something in the system is moving and the vehicles through which deep work can happen.

Many of us share a very human resistance to change, complicated by our mental models, mistaken facticity, and ingrained dominance, superiority, and/or inferiority. In the face of change, transition, and uncertainty, we do not always rise to our best selves. This chapter explores some of the challenges we can encounter as we guide change processes and how consultants can recognize and work with them to support transformation toward more just ways of working and being.

## Conflict with Care

Like many others, my socialized impulse is to slink under the table at the first whiff of conflict. Despite my training in conflict resolution, earlier in my career I would feel a pit in my stomach when conflict was present in a group. My head got foggy, my heart pounded, and the sides of my body tingled.

I found ways to just happen not to notice conflicts, even when they were right in front of me. I'd skate over uncomfortable issues that emerged, even if they were important. You can guess how that usually went: seemingly fine in the short term. Sometimes there was palpable relief that we had dodged a bullet. But the costs were significant, avoiding real and important matters. Issues seldom resolved themselves on their own, and small pebbles irritated their way to big blisters.

Conflict avoidance is so pervasive in dominant US culture that many think it's normal. Yet not telling each other our truths can have deeply harmful consequences.

I have been learning for many years to embrace conflict as a fundamental part of the human experience. It turns out to be essential for creativity, innovation, and transformation. We must break through the limitations of our current understandings to embrace new possibilities, as a seedling must break through its own pod and the surface of the earth to become a plant. Care-full conflict (conflict navigated with care for the humans involved) is essential for growth.

Our mental models, grounded in lived experience and informed by our identities, can conflate conflict with violence, dominance, and irreparable ruptures in relationships.

Steven Brion-Meisels was famous for always wearing a button on his ever-present sport jacket with a quote from Reverend Dr. Martin Luther King, Jr.: "True peace is not merely the absence of tension: it is the presence of justice." A copy of this button hangs above my desk to remind me of Steven and all I learned from him, including the genuine possibility that humans can move through conflict in healthy ways that build connection and the value of embracing non-violent conflict as an act of justice.

Conflict can trigger our fight, flight, freeze, and appease responses. We may feel like it is a threat to our very existence. In the face of conflict, we can lose access to the fullness of ourselves and the inner resources that enable us to consider others' well-being, not just tend to our own survival. Current psychological research and polyvagal theory teach us about the neurological mechanisms by which this happens, giving context to the intensity of our lived experiences.

Organizational conflict often shows up as interpersonal. We think specific people just don't get along. However, I have found that the root of most interpersonal conflicts in the workplace isn't personalities that don't mesh. There are people we click with more than others and rare people with true nefarious intent. But that's not usually what's going on.

Most conflicts arise because we have divergent beliefs, understandings, and ways of living with the forces and factors discussed in previous chapters: racism and systemic oppression, power, decision-making and roles, culture, priorities, and Guiding Ideas. When we behave on the basis of our assumptions about these and don't try to understand why others are behaving differently — in ways we may see as annoying at best and harmful at worst — the result is misunderstanding, othering, and fractured relationships.

Conflict in organizations is an opportunity to bring to the surface what is present below it: the issues, likely outside our awareness, that impact people and impede organizational effectiveness. It is also an opportunity to build awareness and skills to deepen authentic relationships and hold people accountable for the impact of their behaviors.

When my daughter Sasha was 3, she never wanted to wear socks. There was a small battle every morning as I insisted, and she resisted. I brought our dilemma to her brilliant nursery school teacher, Beth.

"Why do you want her to wear socks?" Beth asked.

I didn't want her feet to be cold, of course.

"When is it warm enough for her to go without socks?" she asked.

"Around 50 degrees, I guess."

Beth presented a solution that changed our lives. She suggested a "Sock Wheel" with a dial: on one side over 50 degrees and no socks, under 50 degrees and socks on the other.

Each morning we checked the temperature and moved the dial on the Sock Wheel together. It told us what to do. And like magic, there was no more struggle! We had clarified the terms and expectations and agreed to abide by them. The Sock Wheel took our conflict out of the interpersonal realm. We both understood the criteria by which a decision would be made and became partners in listening to what the wheel said. Most importantly, through that experience, I learned how to be in a deeper partnership with my young child, making sure her needs were met, not taking away her control over her own body, and helping her to understand why some decisions are necessary.

Unsurprisingly, listening is the primary skill for moving through conflict in ways that can surface and heal underlying issues. Deep, mindful listening. Not hearing for the sake of honing our response or retort but listening to remember that this person with whom we are in conflict is a human being saying things that matter to them. This can be hard to do, and it is essential for bringing to light the lack of clarity and shared understanding around the organizational forces that generally underlie conflict.

When conflict is present, we need to slow down and listen to the people who most annoy, anger, or enrage us. We need to learn the source of our divergent understandings and what matters to each of us. We also need to be willing to speak our truth.

Mediation theory frames our underlying motivations as our *interests*, distinct from our *positions*, the strategies we use to meet our interests. When we can figure out together how to hold our divergent views and interests with dignity, we have transformed conflict, regardless of whether we arrive at a solution.

If the people in a conflict are willing, third parties like facilitators and mediators can help them move through their triggered state, listen, and be accountable for their actions. As facilitators, our rigorous listening and attention open up space for others to listen. We are the symbolic Sock Wheel. We do this with our tone, calm presence, breath, and clear, bounded processes. Our confidence in participants' humanity in the moment of conflict creates an invitation to move toward deeper understanding and relationship.

The Neighborhood Sustenance Project (NSP) was a ten-year-old food justice organization in a small city with a lot of poverty and food insecurity. They ran three highly valued programs: an urban farm, an education program for backyard and community garden growers, and an out-of-school-time youth growers program in which young people managed a farmers market and sold the food they grew at a low cost. The directors of these programs were Charity, a Black woman; Amanda, a white woman; and Amor, a woman who had immigrated from the Philippines as a child. All three had been at NSP for over five years. They had worked well together for the first few years, but tensions had recently started rising and tempers had flared more than once.

I had worked with NSP on strategic planning a few years earlier and had developed strong, trusted relationships with everyone on the staff. The executive director, Marianna, a white woman, asked me if I would facilitate a series of conversations for them. I asked her to check with Charity, Amanda, and Amor to make sure they were comfortable having me, a white woman, facilitate their conversations. They were. It is worth noting that I have asked this same question in other instances where people have appreciated the opportunity to bring in a facilitator who is Black, Indigenous, or another person of color instead.

I spoke with Charity, Amanda, Amor, and Marianna individually. It wasn't clear to me if Marianna should be part of the larger conversations or if I needed to facilitate 1:1 conversations between any two of them before they all came together. Charity, Amanda, and Amor all wanted to meet as a group, and they wanted Marianna to participate.

When I spoke with them individually, the three Program Directors each told me how much they loved their work and how proud they were to be a part of NSP. However, they were also frustrated and sad. They each reported feeling disrespected by their colleagues and felt they could no longer depend on each other. While they all loved Marianna, they thought she didn't provide what was needed to change the situation. They all had the same solution: Marianna needed to help the other two change their behaviors.

I opened our first session together by sharing the common themes I had heard in our conversations and my observations and experiences from our previous work together. "I'm honored to be with you and holding you as you move through these conversations. You are each doing an amazing service in the community that makes a difference in people's lives," I began, looking to establish how much I respected and trusted each of them. "When I spoke with each of you, I again heard how committed you are to NSP. And yet, as happens with humans, you are in a challenging moment. I know what good will and good intentions you are bringing to this process and also that harm has taken place and there is hurt present."

I welcomed them each to close their eyes and take a few deep breaths together. "The work we are doing here is really important, and it may feel difficult to enter," I said. "You may have some feelings or be stimulated at some points. Remember that we can always come back to our breath to bring us back into our bodies and the room together, and we can always take a break whenever you need it."

We then developed some agreements for the conversations. "What do you each need us all to agree to so you can show up in this space as openly as you can?" I asked.

"I need to know that I'll be listened to all the way through what I am saying," Amor said. "Sometimes, when we're talking, I don't get to finish my thoughts."

I took a breath to make sure she was complete in her offering. "Thank you for saying that, Amor, that's really important. Would it be okay if we said, 'Check to make sure people are done speaking, and don't speak over each other?'" Amor nodded her head, and I wrote on a flip chart "I want to ensure everyone is committed to staying in the conversation," Marianna added.

"Stay present in the conversation and in the room. Be present for all sessions," I wrote. "Does this capture what you meant?" I asked Marianna.

"Yes, good," she replied.

"Is there anything else?" I asked after a quiet minute.

"I want to make sure nobody's going to be telling everyone about what we say here," Charity said.

"Keep what's said here confidential," I wrote, looking at Charity, who gave a thumbs up.

"What about continuing the conversations outside of this space?" I asked.

"I'm good with that," Amanda said.

"Me too. Anytime y'all want to talk, I'm good," added Amor.

"No, that doesn't work for me," said Charity. "That's part of the problem. Everyone calls me, texts me, and wants to talk all the time. There are no boundaries on anything. I have little kids, and I can't just drop everything and talk."

Amanda and Marianna looked at the floor.

"Oh, that makes sense," Amor said. "Thank you for saying that."

"I imagine we'll talk a lot more about what works well and what doesn't work so well for you in terms of communication. For now, I'm wondering if it would be okay to say 'check for permission before continuing these conversations outside of this space. Be willing to hear 'no,'" I said, looking at Charity to make sure it worked for her.

"Yes, that's good for me. What I need is a boundary to not respond right away or not have to talk about something on the fly if I'm not ready."

"Is there anything else that you need?" I asked again.

"No," they each said.

"Do you want to know more about what anything here means and what you would be agreeing to?" I asked, pointing to the flip chart where I had written the proposed agreements. All shook their heads no. "Is there anything here that you can't or don't want to agree to for any reason?" I asked. Again, all shook their heads no. "Can I see thumbs up that we all agree to these?" Including me, five thumbs went up.

In the process of setting agreements for the conversation, the group had already touched on two key sources of conflict: first, listening fully, and second, timing and consent around conversations. I pointed out that both these issues were rooted in communication styles characteristic of common white organizational ways of being that are often exclusionary for Black, Indigenous, and other people of color. They all nodded. I noted that they were already speaking truths, listening carefully, and honoring each other's needs.

We then began a circle process (see Tools and Resources) that would continue throughout three sessions. This process allowed each person to speak in turn and receive the full listening attention of the rest of the group without interruption or debate. Each woman spoke of her disappointment and frustration, what didn't work for her, and the impact it had on her.

I introduced them to the Conflict Avoidance Escalator, a framework I developed to show how conflict avoidance creates fractures (see Tools and Resources). It helped them see how their inability to speak the truth about what they needed had led to misunderstanding. This was particularly true for the Black and Filipino-American women who had worked hard to accommodate white culture at a considerable cost to their emotional well-being.

"When you text me at all hours, and I'm home with my kids, I assume it's an emergency, and I need to attend to it immediately. It's disruptive to my family and me. If it really is an emergency, that's fine. Otherwise, why can't it wait till my regular hours?" Charity said during the second conversation.

"Thank you for saying that," Marianna said. "I didn't know that. I grew up inside organizations that did that; I thought it was normal. Now that you say this, I can see how disrespectful it can feel. I won't do that anymore."

It could have been easy for them to remain in conflict. However, because of their ability to fully listen, each saw how her own behavior had exacerbated the situation, causing tension to escalate. Their honest conversations were sometimes painful, but through careful attention, they restored trust. More than five years later, these women are still working closely together, navigating challenging circumstances and grounding their work together in the trust they were able to restore.

In truth, I often still feel that pit in my stomach when conflict surfaces, but I can also feel the excitement of possibility because the truth can open the door to healing and repair is emerging.

## Anticipate Resistance

People don't hire consultants to help them stay the same, even though that may be (perhaps unconsciously) what they really want. After years of confusion, bafflement, and general annoyance, I am learning to expect resistance in all change processes. How could it be otherwise? Moving through change can feel like an existential crisis in both the immediate and longer term. What will the future hold? Will we continue to survive, to belong in the niche we've occupied? What do you mean I can't behave in ways I am used to behaving? What will be required of me? For many of us, these questions provoke resistance.

Resistance is a wily little critter and has many disguises. There are the classic overt behaviors: publicly questioning or disparaging the process, its internal leaders, or the consultant, particularly when they are women, Black people, Indigenous people, and other people of color. There are also the oh-so-many covert behaviors: agreeing to one thing and then doing the exact opposite, gossiping, not following through on commitments, not showing up to meetings, and on and on. Many of these behaviors are attempts to avoid facing possible discomfort, often grounded in some kind of privilege.

Much as I know better, I still have to manage the part of me that wants to take resistance personally. If I am determined, I can usually find some kind of evidence that it is about me. My job in these cases is to: (1) manage myself to remember that it is not about me — it's about the system and how people have been socialized to believe they are entitled to comfort and dominance; (2) listen for the grains of truth inside of resistance, as Deep Democracy teaches, and ask myself if is there some wisdom in the resistance that could be helpful to the system or the change process; and (3) see resistance as a sign of movement in the system.

Noticing resistance is an opportunity to foster continued opening into new awareness. It requires careful attention, compassion, and practice to distinguish the wisdom in resistance from the behaviors rooted in fear, dominance, or disenfranchisement that we are trying to undo. I try to notice how behaviors impact me, a practice some consultants call "self as instrument." Tuning into my feelings and sensations in my body can give me information about what may lie beneath the behaviors.

My colleague and I were in the cafeteria of the Peaceful Pathways School, waiting for the 25 staff and faculty members to arrive. Over the past few years, interpersonal tensions had grown high in the face of a sustained leadership vacuum, lack of organizational direction, and lots of role confusion. The board had hired us, a white consultant team, to work with the overwhelmingly white staff to restore organizational health. We interviewed most of the staff and had a pretty clear assessment of the situation. The purpose of this meeting was to initiate the process we would be in together over the next several months. The desired outcomes were for staff to develop a shared understanding of the findings in our assessment and begin to be in dialogue with each other as a step toward building relationships and trust.

We greeted people warmly and introduced ourselves as they trickled slowly in. We heard a lot of things like "Let's see what you think of us...." and "You must have a headache from everything you heard!" There was curiosity and interest about what we had found — and also palpable anxiety which I could feel in my chest.

Soon after everyone sat down and the new principal, Maria, welcomed the group, Carmen raised her hand. With a suspicious tone, she asked why Tom was missing. Had he been excluded? Maria answered matter-of-factly that he was having car trouble and was on his way. Then my colleague and I stood up to begin the day. Right away, there was a question from Greg about the arrangement of the room. Why were the chairs in a circle and not around tables? More issues and questions arose. When would the break be, Kitty wondered. Libby suddenly needed to run out for an errand that just couldn't wait.

"I'm noticing a lot of concerns and questions," I said, naming what I saw happening. "I imagine some of you might be a little nervous to hear what we heard in our assessment. Let's get to it." The questions stopped, and after we did some opening activities, folks settled in to listen.

I used to see these kinds of behaviors as rude expressions of privilege and entitlement. But while privilege and entitlement are still omnipresent, I have come to see the skepticism and defeatism that underlie resistance as the defenses of tender hearts that don't want to be broken or disappointed yet again. This perspective gives me empathy when I encounter the challenging behaviors resistance engenders and helps me hold people accountable.

The best strategy I have found for working with resistance is naming it, openly and compassionately, without blame. This entails a delicate balance between hearing concerns, incorporating useful input, and not letting myself be distracted by unfounded fears and habits born of socialized dominance.

Myrna Lewis, the co-founder of Deep Democracy, a comprehensive group facilitation methodology (see Tools and Resources), says that "you've got to kiss people over the edge," meaning we need to invite people gently and lovingly into new territory. I have seen "kissing people over the edge" catalyze profound positive transformation. But sometimes the resistance was too strong and could not be moved. In reflecting on those times, I wonder if I was not in a place of compassion and equanimity and the energy of my impatience contributed to resistance. It isn't easy to find the middle path, as the Buddhists call it, the exact balance of honoring the truth of what is and holding out the possibility of change that lets people accept the invitation into the process.

I've learned a lot about handling resistance from Deep Democracy, which offers a brilliant question for people who are reluctant to participate or agree to something: "What do you need to come along?" This question invites what Deep Democracy calls "The wisdom in the 'NO!'" to emerge. There is usually what they call a "grain of truth" in resistance and reluctance, though it can be shrouded under challenging behaviors and therefore hard to recognize. Surfacing previously missed concerns can be helpful to both the process and the individuals involved, whether or not they end up impacting the decision.

I like to imagine people in organizational change processes as kernels of popcorn in a pot. As we sit more fully and compassionately in our current truth and possible futures, the pot heats up, and the popping starts. First one, then two. Then a few more. Then the bulk of the kernels burst. When the popping finishes, there are inevitably a few kernels that just never popped.

I have heard it said that in change efforts, one third of the people will be fully on board, one third will eventually come along as the culture shifts and carries them, and one third just won't be able to shift. That's not a scientific number, but you get the idea. This framing helps me let go of expecting everyone to change (pop) at the same pace. Some people are just not ready.

For transformation work to take root, resistance can't be passed over. But neither should it be given unwarranted power to derail processes.

## Discomfort and Uncertainty

*The unknown is where all outcomes are possible, enter
it with grace.*

— author unknown

Sometime in my early twenties, I read this line in a mystery novel: "If A is right, B is not wrong either." This one sentence in a book whose title I can no longer recall took my breath away and shifted how I saw the world. I've heard many consultants speak of both/and solutions — same thing. But it can be challenging for people to move away from binaries that insist there is only one right way and anything else is wrong, particularly for folks in a US context.

In many organizations and for many people, it's hard to say and hear "I don't know," "I don't understand," and most especially "The way forward is uncertain." In most US cultures, there is a high reward for knowing, solving problems, taming chaos and uncertainty, and tying things up into beautiful packages. But superficial beauty may mask a rotten core.

I can get a lot of approbation and ego satisfaction from short-term, transactional wins. A meeting in which nobody feels tension. A completed strategic plan with beautiful graphics that may or may not address community needs. But the long game of justice requires us to have the fortitude, patience, and trust to forgo short-term comfort for long-term change. I am continually learning that discomfort and uncertainty are integral to transformational change.

I sometimes think of my work as managing uncertainty. I am looking to balance creativity, curiosity, and anxiety (mine, my clients' and the generalized anxiety of the world) while not letting fear rule the day when untethered sensations arise.

Insisting on certainty can reinforce the status quo of dominance. Transformation, innovation, and wisdom come when we learn from mistakes, don't rush solutions, and sit with unfinished things.

The refusal to live in complexity and process drives us to embrace quick fixes and overly simplistic solutions that recreate dominance and unsustainability.

The tension between our current reality and our desired state, which Parker Palmer calls "the tragic gap," is inherently uncomfortable. That's the point — for transformation to occur, we must get uncomfortable enough to let go of our current state. Yet we must also maintain enough trust and comfort with our process that people stay in it — but not so much comfort that people feel they have arrived someplace good enough to stop striving.

*When I was nine months pregnant with my first child, I suddenly got very uncomfortable. I had loved being pregnant up until then. I loved feeling the baby inside of me, having her with me everywhere I went, and relishing the moment-to-moment tangible miracle that my body was incubating an entire human being. And then, a week or so before she was born, I hit a wall. I just couldn't sit still in my own skin, and I couldn't for the life of me get comfortable. My wise midwife told me, "That's what's supposed to happen. You need to get uncomfortable, or you will never be able to let go of the pregnancy." After that, the birth could not come fast enough.*

Lev Vygotsky developed the Learning Zone model, which holds that there are the three zones of learning, represented as three concentric circles. Our comfort zone on the inside, in which we are doing things we know how to do, our panic zone on the outside in which we are activated and triggered and cannot grow, and in the middle, a zone of just-right discomfort in which we can stretch and grow.

My friend, Orah Fireman, wisely noted the difference between liberating and oppressive discomfort: "Discomfort can make transformation possible, but outside of relationship, context, and trust, it can silence and catalyze disengagement and divestment."

When we try to avoid discomfort by jumping out of the frying pan, we often end up in the even greater pain of the fire. It is difficult to imagine and breathe into our desired futures when our conditioning prevents us from tolerating the discomfort required to muck around in what Brene Brown calls "the messy middle" that every creative and transformative process must pass through.

"Have we just made things worse?" Roger worried during the closing go-around of a two-hour planning committee meeting.

"I am discouraged; I don't think we're going to be able to do this," Sharon added.

It was the second of four scheduled calls to plan the agenda for a national meeting of elder rights advocates. The planning committee was an earnest group. Many of them had never been part of any planning process before. We had brainstormed and kicked around several ideas but had not yet arrived at a settled place. With the national meeting three months away, we were in the messy middle.

I saw a different picture from the frustration others had voiced. "I think you've just done a magnificent job," I told the group, and I believed it. "People had a lot of interesting ideas. You all listened carefully to each other, and we clarified our purpose and what we want to achieve."

We did not expect that we would make a final decision that day. The pressure to finish the agenda was utterly artificial! We had another meeting already scheduled for just a week later to continue the process, and nothing would stall for lack of a decision at that moment.

We agreed that Phoebe, the committee chair, and I would look over the notes together and come to the next meeting with a distillation of what the group had generated.

As Phoebe and I combed through the notes a few days later, it became clear that despite several obfuscating ideas, there was a clear purpose and desired outcomes for the national meeting, as well as many possible processes we could use. We distilled a draft agenda, pretty confident that it was a good representation of what the group wanted. With the distance of time and a different approach to organizing the notes, we could see what we had not seen before.

On our next committee call the following week, Phoebe presented what we had developed. There were still some minor tweaks and upgrades, but the agenda was clear to everyone. It was an exciting, and I'd go as far as to say transformational, moment. Coming through uncertainty together in a respectful way was a new experience for many of them, and it built trust within the group.

The national meeting was a special and very meaningful event, thanks in no small part to the messy middle we had waded through to develop the right agenda.

For many people, staying in the messy middle can be intolerable. For them, *any* way forward is better than uncertainty. To put an end to the pain, people may rush decisions before they have fully considered all the implications. Hence, Peter Senge warns that, "Today's problems are yesterday's solutions."

A key concept in negotiation is BATNA: your Best Alternative to a Negotiated Agreement. If you don't want to agree to a proposal and might consider walking away, what's your best alternative?

Based on this, I developed the idea of BAPA: Best Alternative to Plan A. If coming to a decision or closure on an issue is Plan A, and discomfort or urgency are dictating a rush to finish, what might be the BAPA? I offer this when people try and force solutions to minimize discomfort and uncertainty. Is there an interim solution we can settle on for now that doesn't lock us into something we'll regret in the future? What, if anything, is the cost of waiting for an action or a decision until we are actually clear about what needs to happen?

Asking about our BAPA gives us time to pause and think about what might be best in the longer term.

The most important thing I can do to facilitate people through discomfort is to manage my own anxiety and regulate my nervous system. Deb Dana, one of the leading thinkers in healing trauma, has said, "Only if I am a regulated resource can

I be a regulated resource for others." If my nervous system is dysregulated and I'm anxious, it is that much harder for me to hold calm and generous space for others.

It takes artful consulting to support the right range of discomfort in service of transformation. This often involves helping people learn to ask deeper questions and wait more patiently for answers. It's a significant shift for many people to become comfortable not knowing and to sit in the "not yet" space even as the world is on fire.

## Overwhelm and Urgency

*There is such urgency in the multitude of crises we face, it can make it hard to remember that in fact it is urgency thinking (urgent constant unsustainable growth) that got us to this point, and that our potential success lies in doing deep, slow, intentional work.*

— adrienne maree brown

Overwhelm and urgency often shape organizational culture. Nearly every organization I see has too many goals and projects, too many moving parts, and people with just far too much to do. This can result in burnt-out and frazzled staff, job dissatisfaction, a toxic workplace, and compromised services and products.

Like a diner at a buffet, organizations sometimes just don't know when or how to say no. And with massively overloaded plates, things fall off.

Here are some factors that make it hard for people to say no:

- Structures and cultures in which saying no is not an option
- Fear of not doing enough to alleviate the suffering they see around them

- Fear of Missing Out (FOMO); the new, shiny, exciting thing can be hard to pass up
- Fear of not being seen as a team player
- Fear of not being seen as effective or hard-working
- Fear of becoming irrelevant or unimportant
- Fear of slowing down and possibly succumbing to laziness
- Fear of disappointing (e.g., colleagues, customers, clients, other stakeholders)
- Fear of losing face with funders or even losing funds

Sometimes we really can't say no, and sometimes we can but our fears get in the way. Our fears are not all grounded in mistaken facticity — external and internal pressures are often very real.

What is the source of all this fear? Capitalism, patriarchy, and white dominance all survive by convincing us that we are not good enough as we are and that we are only as valuable as what we produce and consume. Our internalized voices can do an excellent job of keeping us in a state of fear, believing that we are never doing enough.

The US Surgeon, General Vivek Murthy, articulated a question that has been on my mind for a long time: *How can we tilt toward love and away from fear?* Stepping off the hamster wheel created by the cultural drives of *more, more, more* and *never good enough* is really hard. Everywhere we turn, there are so many messages that reinforce this fear. And some of us face genuine threats: risk of stakeholder suffering, losing funding, losing status, losing position. But internalized voices can obscure the ability to tell real threats from imagined ones.

Resmaa Menakem's book about racialized trauma, *My Grandmother's Hands*, is one of those books I want us to shut down the world to read — and not start up again until we've all metabolized it. It is full of important pieces of information and helpful practices, including the powerful observation that "The central feature of any trauma response is speed."

I try to help my clients see their sense of urgency and the sheer volume of their workload as symptomatic of the trauma of white dominance culture. People try to outrun the pain of dehumanization and prove their worth through productivity. When I introduce this idea to clients, their response is usually some degree of relief — the phenomenon has a name and cause. However, many are also sure that their situation is an exception and there is no way it can change. I coach clients to distinguish between actual threats and fears that emerge from mistaken facticity, or what many have called FEAR: False Evidence Appearing Real.

Stepping outside of our addiction to urgency and learning to tell what really does need our attention right now can be challenging and scary. We fear we will fail and miss important things.

I see a useful distinction between urgency and alacrity. Our internalized urgency tells us that everything needs to happen now or catastrophe may ensue. Alacrity allows us to respond swiftly to things that require an immediate response, recognizing that not everything does.

It is helpful to look at workload as an equation. I developed this formula based on a similar one I learned from the Rockwood Leadership Institute. Capacity (leadership, time available, resources, skills) sits on one side, Expectations (goals, deadlines) on the other. If the two sides don't balance, the quality of work can deteriorate and people will suffer as they pedal harder to keep up, haunted by a continual sense of failure. We can reduce overwhelm by adding or removing things on one side or the other until they balance.

A few years ago, I finally got rid of the chain link fence that ran along the side of my yard, separating my property from my neighbors. Then I got bold and removed two large forsythias that had been in the yard since we moved in more than a decade earlier. Though I love forsythia, I had never really liked them there. A year later, I got inspired and hacked three manicured azaleas down to the nub so they could grow into their natural shapes. Then I planted Bee Balm, Echinacea, and Asiatic Lilies, a couple of butterfly bushes, bulbs for the springtime, and dahlias for summer.

Neighbors stop by now and tell me how much they appreciate my garden. It has transformed from a dull and awkward yard to something beautiful, even as it is still a work in progress. The secret lies in what I took away — which let other things bloom.

When we always say yes and respond to calls to jump by asking how high, the result is often overwhelm and overload, which make it hard for us to follow through on our commitments. I present my clients with the idea that every no is a yes to something else. I encourage them to see that removing things opens space for other things to flourish, for creative new directions, or even just for working more effectively on existing projects and tasks. Many people find this process excruciatingly hard for all the reasons discussed earlier. But for chronically overwhelmed people, the positive impact of working more thoughtfully and intentionally can be life changing.

The story that follows illustrates how I used conflict resolution and deep listening processes to help a group recognize and transform their ways of being around overwhelm and urgency (for more about the processes, see Tools and Resources).

The six-woman management team from Hungry No More, a community food security and distribution non-profit, had gathered for a two-day retreat to further develop their already cohesive team. Things were off to a good start: the mood was relaxed and people were visibly happy to be together in such a beautiful setting.

The retreat started with some words of welcome from Sal, the ED, and a few moments of breathing together in silence to center ourselves. As the facilitator, I introduced a little context, the retreat POP, the agreements they had previously set, and our opening go-around to hear what each person was looking forward to over the next two days and what they needed to let go of to be fully present.

We next used a circle process to hear from each person about how things were going for them with the team. Speaking in turn, everyone had as much time as she wanted to say what was on her mind and heart about their work while her colleagues listened without comment.

As we went around the circle there was a common theme of appreciation: "I love working with you all."

"I'm so honored to be part of this team." "There's no place else I would want to be but here." It was beautiful to witness.

We then did another go-around and a different theme began to emerge, one that I knew was present from my earlier 1:1 conversations with each team member. Some members of the team believed that the best way for the organization to operate was to respond to all opportunities and requests. Others believed they should slow down and operate more deliberately and strategically. The team had not talked much about this issue, fearing the conflict it might engender. They were in what Deep Democracy calls a "polarity," two positions that seem to be opposites, but which are actually part of the same continuum. In my opening remarks, I had noted this polarity as a key challenge for them.

"I am overwhelmed with the amount of work I have," Jodi offered, beginning the second go-around. "I never know what my priorities should be."

"I always feel I'm letting you all down" said Ava, discussing her overwhelm with the volume of work.

"It's hard for me to keep track of everything, there's just so much," Becky said, as she described the impact on her sleep and energy.

Sal offered her appreciation for how hard everyone on the team worked and how much they cared: "Our partners and clients appreciate us and think so highly of our work, and it's because we are so responsive. I feel overwhelmed too, but I think there really isn't a choice — we need to respond or people won't get their needs met."

Julia, the Deputy Director nodded in agreement and echoed Sal's words when it was her turn: "I am so proud of this team and how well we rock it. I'm sad that people feel so overwhelmed. I wish that wasn't the case."

I again posed to the team that this was a key polarity in their work together. All agreed that it was a big issue. "How about we use this polarity, not as right or wrong, nor to convince each other, but just to understand where you are?" I asked. They were all very interested.

After a delicious lunch, we began the afternoon session. I again reiterated the polarity and checked that it rang true and important for them. Yes, for sure. Then I checked in on their agreements that they wanted to listen and see things in new ways. An emphatic yes all around. I described the process we would use, which is based on Deep Democracy tools. This process is only used once a group has collectively identified a polarity and agreed to examine it together.

We drew a line down the center of the room. On one side of the line was one end of the polarity: "We need to always be responsive to meet people's needs." On the other side was the other end of the polarity: "We will be more effective and sustainable if we slow down and operate more deliberately and strategically." Rather than arguing, this method allows people to simply represent and advocate a position. There is no defending or protesting. We all started on one side of the line, facing the empty space on the other side. Everyone had to explain why it was important to always be responsive. Even if it was not someone's primary position, they still found reasons to advocate for it.

When we were done, the whole group moved to the other side of the line and spoke to the empty space where we had just been. They all explained why slowing down and being more strategic was important to them, even if it wasn't their primary position. Then people were free to move back and forth across the line, advocating for one position or the other. Several people said seemingly contradictory things when they were on different sides of the line.

On one side, Sandy offered, "If we don't strike while the iron is hot, we will miss a lot of important opportunities," and on the other, she noted that "When we go slower, we do better work." Eventually she said, "I can't keep up the fast pace, I'll have to leave if things don't change."

Everyone continued moving back and forth until they had said everything they had to say.

After a break, we gathered again and I asked the incredibly helpful Deep Democracy question: "What grains of truth did you hear?" This question allows people the space to back away from the need to advocate for a position and turn their attention to the essential truths the exercise has surfaced.

"I heard how tired everyone is and how unsustainable the pace is," Sal said sadly.

Jodi said, "I heard how much satisfaction everyone gets from making sure everyone in our community has food to eat."

"I heard how much nobody wants to let anybody down," Julia said.

"I heard that we treat everything like it's urgent and the house is on fire, but sometimes that's not true," said Becky.

The grains of truth kept coming. Each team member had multiple insights.

Their newfound depth of clarity made it relatively easy for them to determine how they could put their insights into action. They all agreed they needed to act more strategically so they could meet their community's needs. They agreed to spend time at the retreat developing a Strategy Filter to identity criteria they could use to decide when requests needed an urgent response (see Tools and Resources). They also agreed to practice reality testing whether requests were absolutely urgent and to come back together in a month to see if anything had changed.

## When to Act and When to Pause

*You can't push a stream to flow, but if you remove the blockages it will flow by itself.*

— Adam Kahane

*When we pause, allow a gap and breathe deeply, we can experience instant refreshment. Suddenly, we slow down, look out, and there's the world.*

— Pema Chödrön

*Do you have the patience to wait*
*until your mud settles,*
*and the water is clear?*
*Can you remain unmoving*
*until the right action*
*arises by itself?*

— Lao Tzu

In the US we have a cultural bias for action over planning and reflection. Capitalism and the dominance ideology that drives it tell us our very worth is measured by what we produce. We tend to believe that as long as we're moving, we are on the right path. It is easy, as Ben Franklin warned, to "confuse action with progress."

Action bias is a danger for consultants, and I can find myself battling its lure. Organizations engage me because they are

143

looking for a result. It is very compelling to want to prove to my clients that their valuable resources and trust have been well placed and they haven't made a mistake by hiring me.

Questioning the pace of a change process is excellent fuel for self-doubt. But I know that healing is not a quick fix, and self-doubt can get in the way of honest reflection.

I am committed to what I believe creates real change: acting with care guided by reflection, deep listening to inner wisdom, sitting together in our shared truth, moving at the speed of trust and dignity, and lifting up the needs and voices of folks who have been historically excluded. Action for its own sake may stoke my ego in the short term, but it isn't necessarily in my client's best interest. Real change moves at a human pace.

I'm not known among my loved ones as a patient person. And yet I continue to learn about the profound power of doing nothing when action is not needed, listening for the wisdom and learning in pausing, and taking action only when it is required.

I had consulted on and off for a few years with Community and Carrots, an organization devoted to promoting local food and agriculture. The executive director, Rose, called one day to tell me they wanted to have a board retreat, though she didn't know why. Maybe to do some planning? It wasn't clear.

Rose and I chatted to catch up. I was eager to hear how she and the organization were doing in the few years since we'd last worked together. "I have no idea why the board wants a retreat, and I don't think it's the right thing for us right now," she said. "Everything is going well. We've achieved all the big things we set out to do. We've grown so much, and now we need to catch up to ourselves. We need to live in our new skin for a while before we see what's next."

"That sounds amazing," I said, impressed and inspired but not surprised by all they had accomplished.

"We've never been in a better position. Programmatically, financially, staff-wise, things are better than they have ever been," she continued. "But things between the board and I have never been so difficult! I've never had this experience with the board in all my years here." She was near tears. "They are demanding so many things that just don't make any sense for us right now."

I met with Rose and Caitlin, the board chair, to try and tease out the purpose of a retreat. Caitlin insisted that she wanted a retreat but could not identify a clear purpose or desired outcomes. "If there's no purpose," I told them, "there's no reason to have a retreat. But something's going on here. Let's figure out what's going on, and then we can figure out what to do about it."

Caitlin, Rose, and I met with the rest of the board's executive committee. We used a listening circle process. Our purpose was to determine what was true about where they were and where they wanted to be. They all acknowledged how much the organization had grown and how much there was to celebrate. They also agreed that there was tension. However, the board members seemed to think things needed to keep moving forward faster and Rose was blocking them.

Rose expressed her dismay at the board's dissatisfaction and the different things they thought they were doing to help the organization, which were in fact creating difficulty and challenges for the staff. She explained that she thought what they needed to do at this point was let the dust settle and live in their new home, new size, and current goals before setting new goals and starting new programs, which was what the board wanted. Slowing down and listening to what was actually going on in the organization was a radical idea for the board members.

Caitlin had a big aha. "Oh dear!" she said, "I've been so busy trying to solve problems that I haven't paid attention to what I'm solving for. I've been solving the wrong problems!" A brilliant piece of insight.

As I reflected what I was hearing, they came to understand that the board had felt useful during the period of expansion and had thrived on the excitement. They wanted to keep up that pace. "You've done an amazing job," I told them, "but that intense expansion is not what the organization needs now. In line with your values and philosophy around sustainable agriculture, Rose would like to slow down the pace of change, perhaps just for a while, and see where you are before setting your sights on new goals."

Everyone on the executive committee could see the unintentional harm that pushing to continue expanding at a fast clip had caused Rose and the staff. They saw they had put the organization at risk as their brilliant executive director was eyeing the door under the pressure.

They decided upon an extended board meeting with the staff to celebrate all their successes, hear Rose's vision for the coming year, and identify how the board could contribute. This was an important step toward restoring their frayed trust and reassuring the board that the organization was on the right track and they were fulfilling their governance role.

I often need to deliberately slow groups down in their process so they can reflect and come into relationship with where they are and what is true. When urgency calls us to speed up, we easily forget to be human and connect with each other. We need to slow down long enough to connect with the truth of where we are, what action is needed now, and all that could be possible. This can be particularly hard when there is time pressure and many things are moving quickly. But there's a reason *go slow to go fast* is a common facilitator refrain.

I help my clients consider the potential consequences of slowing down and moving too quickly. I also support them to notice when they are stuck and move toward wise action with alacrity when needed.

My most important tool for helping clients discern when it may be time to pause is understanding and noticing my own urgency and action bias. My ability to slow down and regulate my breathing and nervous system allows me to recognize when we all may need to slow down and pause.

It takes time to build the muscle to slow down. Spiritual practice, meditation, yoga, and lots of time outdoors and with plants have all become essential for me in learning how to do this.

# 7

# Creating Meaningful Meetings

*It's very hard to hate someone if you look them in the
eye and recognize them as a human being.*
— Maya Angelou

My college application asked me to write an essay exploring the question, "Do the ends justify the means?" Teenage me was clear: NO, NO, NO! The ends NEVER justify the means! The energy and mindset with which we do something shapes the very thing itself. What feels like several lifetimes later, I see more nuance in this question, though I do still believe that our processes are inextricable from the results they produce.

I spend much of my time planning, preparing for, and facilitating meetings. Meetings are central vehicles through which much organizational work happens. By meeting, I mean any time two or more people are engaged in purposeful work or conversation. This includes retreats, mediations, workshops, training, and work sessions.

A lot of factors contribute to the success, fizzle, or flow of meetings. Many of them are developed before a meeting even starts in what facilitators often call *setting the container*, that is, shaping the context for the meeting itself. The elements of containers — agenda design, space, tone, logistics — are frequently invisible to participants.

In this chapter I will consider meeting containers, what they are and how to create them. Chapter 8, the next and final chapter, will explore the other critical ingredient for successful meetings: skillful facilitation. Please note that both these chapters emerge from and are aimed at meetings in the progressive and mostly non-profit US context where I do the bulk of my work.

# Alignment

*Everything is energy and that is all there is to it. Match the frequency of the reality you want and you cannot help but get that reality. It can be no other way. This is not philosophy. This is physics.*

— Albert Einstein

In my early twenties I spent a few weeks at the Findhorn Foundation, a spiritual community and learning center in Northern Scotland. There I first encountered the magic of group transformation. Before any kind of gathering, from a workshop session to dish crew or dinner, there was what they called an attunement. Everyone involved gathered in a circle, held hands, closed their eyes, and focused on aligning their energies — within themselves, with each other, and with the task at hand. I had never seen anything like this before, and it made me uncomfortable. After a little while, however, I came to love it. I loved how it felt in my body as well as the sense of belonging and purpose it invited me into several times a day. When I came home, I longed for it.

An energetic field is created when we gather together. Just as we must nurture individual inner well-being, we must attend to the energetic alignment of groups and organizations. We communicate through so much more than words and body language. As energetic beings connected with all of life, we read, sense, and influence each other, even remotely. Yet we're usually not aware of how we are being shaped by each other and the situations and roles we find ourselves in. Ron Heifetz likens us to violin strings: when you pluck one, the others begin to vibrate.

We all have our own energetic fields that radiate beyond our bodies (this isn't just me talking; as Einstein said, this is physics!). When we come together, our energies can align and generate life-giving creativity. They can also collide or repel, which causes all kinds of negative outcomes including disengagement, oppression, and harm. When we attend to group alignment, we make space for the emergence of synergy and collaboration. Recent research about trauma and the nervous system confirms that alignment practices also help us co-regulate ourselves, enabling us to be more present with what is happening now.

I always include some kind of alignment practice in meetings. Whether I am explicit about what I'm doing or why depends upon the culture of the group.

It was an unseasonably warm and sunny early spring day. My colleague and I were in a lovely rustic retreat center facilitating a team development retreat for the staff of a public health agency.

We could sense the reluctance as we began the day. Folks greeted each other with friendly hellos, but many sat alone, reading through the materials we had prepared as they waited for the session to begin.

My colleague and I checked in and agreed we needed to add more time for icebreakers. These are (usually) short activities that help folks warm up to each other and the meeting. After introducing ourselves and the POP, we moved everyone outside where we facilitated a series of 1:1 conversations with different prompts, including some funny ones. We gave people an opportunity to speak with almost everyone else in the group. When we returned inside, the mood was palpably lighter.

The tone set by the icebreaker conversations sustained throughout the day. The group was able to move through some difficult moments with grace and care and ended on a very high note, having met all their goals.

Tools I use to create energetic alignment in groups include:

- Starting meetings with silence, mindful breathing, or guided meditation
- Check-ins*
- Meeting Guidelines*
- Simple stretches, body movements, dancing together at breaks, as appropriate for the accessibility needs and culture of the group
- Sharing food
- Sharing stories about our lives, experiences, and challenges
- Sharing our longings and dreams
- Group singing
- Taking a breath together when things speed up faster than we want them to be
- Icebreakers or quick games that allow a group to laugh together at transition moments like returning from breaks
- Playing music during breaks or transition moments

*See Tools and Resources

## Pre-Meeting Planning

Effective meetings foster a sense of belonging and connection, whether they are virtual or in person. Creating trustworthy containers that invite participants to shed armor and risk vulnerability starts way before we get "in the room."

In her groundbreaking book *Emergent Strategy*, adrienne maree brown calls for "more presence, less prep." I agree that presence is essential. To the degree that preparation and plans constrain our ability to be present, they're not helpful. At the same time, thoughtful preparation implemented with flexibility and grace is key to creating spaces of generative creativity that hold the possibility of operating outside of dominant and oppressive dynamics.

I always co-create meetings and retreats with my clients to ensure that the processes we use will meet them where they are and move them forward. Co-creation ensures that the meeting will be culturally appropriate and inviting. It also builds shared ownership for our work. Whatever the nature and scope of the engagement, size of the group, or number of people involved in the planning, we still plan together.

Here are some of the questions that guide our planning:

- What is the POP (Purpose, Outcomes, Process) for the meeting?
- What tone or feeling do we want the meeting to have (e.g., intimate and vulnerable, more formal, etc.)?
- Where is the group relative to their desired outcomes?
- What kind of preparation does the meeting require? This might include research to bring in factual data, an opinion survey, or critical conversations to resolve issues between people who will be participating.
- What kind of space or facility will be most conducive to our goals?
- What kind of invitation and information will set a welcoming environment for a good, creative gathering (e.g.., how people will be invited, what kind of preparation they will do in advance)?
- How will we create a sense of belonging and enthusiasm for the participants?
- What additional activities will support connection and relationship building (e.g., meals, games, hikes, etc.)?
- What roles will different people play in planning and at the event?

I use the responses to these questions to design an agenda for the planning group's feedback. I find the POP model (Purpose, Outcome, Process) essential for planning meeting agendas in the US context where I work (see Tools and Resources). I believe a complete agenda needs to state WHY the meeting is happening (purpose), WHAT we hope to accomplish (outcomes), and the Processes we will use to achieve our desired outcomes.

Identifying a meeting's purpose and desired outcomes can be a process in and of itself, as they can shift several times during planning. However, getting clear on them is paramount, as everything else flows from there. We keep refining until the agenda is right. This may take one conversation or multiple rounds of back and forth. Generally, the higher the stakes of the meeting, the more involved the planning.

People often say there just isn't enough time, particularly in meetings. It can also be true that there's too much time, and meetings drag on and on.

How much time do you need for a meeting? Ideally, the POP determines the length of a meeting, but there are a few other factors:

- What processes will be required to reach the desired outcomes, and how much time will they take?
- How much time is available? What will create enough time and space for good work without overly taxing participants?
- What will best fit the language and culture of the group? Facilitating meetings with simultaneous translation takes additional time. Some cultural contexts require more time for people to speak and make personal connections.
- What are the group's norms around the use of time? Do they start and end on time? Are they comfortable with flexibility?

Meetings are just milestones in overall processes. Not everything needs to or can be accomplished in meetings. Overpacked agendas are as common as mosquitos in the summer in Maine. The most obvious cure for addressing limited time is to adjust the desired outcomes accordingly. It's simple math. The aspiration needs to match the context and the time available; we need to balance and adjust both sides of the equation to make it work.

Different cultures hold time and punctuality very differently. I'm continuing to learn not to impose my commitment to punctuality and schedules while still honoring my commitment to finish meetings on time so people can meet their subsequent obligations. This is challenging, and I have no magic formula to offer. I simply try my best to listen with respect and to hold as sacred both the desired outcomes the group is reaching for and the different ways members of the group hold time. As facilitator, we can't always control when the meeting starts, but we can usually determine when it ends.

It is important to make sure that all participants understand and agree to the POP. Ideally this happens when they receive and respond to the meeting invite, but at the very minimum we need to attend to it at the start of the meeting. One way we set the tone for meetings is by sending agendas and preparation materials in advance. These communications should include a warm welcome and information about what folks will need to do to prepare, and they should be sent with enough time for people to complete pre-meeting tasks. However, more is not always better. I have seen organizations send out literal tomes to board members in advance of meetings. Chock full of information, the useful mixed with the excessive, these books are practically an invitation not to read! I encourage my clients to send just the right amount of material to get people excited and help them be informed. Not an ounce more. Sometimes an email with a question to ponder in advance is enough.

I sometimes talk with individual participants before meetings to hear their hopes, needs, and interests. This is particularly useful when there is conflict present. These conversations can help participants build trust in me and the process and help me determine how best to hold the space. It can sometimes be helpful for planning committee members to reach out to participants in advance to welcome them individually and help them understand what will happen in the meeting.

I have heard from colleagues and clients, particularly Black, Indigenous, and other people of color, what a relief it is to come into a meeting and know what to expect. I am continuing to learn how exhausting and demoralizing it is to attend to the invisible and obscure rules of the dominant culture that do not honor the full human range of ways of being and knowing. One way we can alleviate some of this exhaustion is by being transparent as well as welcoming.

My long-term client Celeste, a Black woman, and I were meeting in person about an upcoming planning session for her department. We'd been working together on and off for the better part of ten years. I'd facilitated several processes and retreats for the department she led and coached her as she assumed new leadership roles. She often spoke of how much she enjoyed working together and the profound sense of synergy she felt.

I pulled out my computer to take notes and said, "I'm just pulling out my computer to take notes."

She replied, "Thank you for telling me. I would wonder what you were doing if you hadn't told me."

I was floored. How could this brilliant woman with whom I had a long and trusted history be confused by such a simple action? It took my breath away. I realized yet again how little I understand the marginalizing experiences of Black, Indigenous, and other people of color and how often I take for granted the behaviors and practices of the dominant culture.

Celeste's courage and honesty in sharing her experience at that moment touched me deeply. She helped me understand better how useful it is to spell out in clear detail why things are happening so people do not have to do mental gymnastics to try and make sense of them through the distortions of racism and other oppressions.

Clearly articulated, predictable meeting containers create inclusion and belonging. They set the stage for enjoyable, connecting, and productive meetings that model the generative and connecting ways humans can work together.

## Agendas

Good meetings have a clear beginning, middle, and end. Too often, people dive right into meetings without a clear POP. It can take some masterful martial arts moves to stay connected to all the ideas and topics flying around! People compete for airtime to make sure their issue gets addressed. The meeting ends abruptly without clear next steps. Time has been spent, but not well.

Think about the arc of a meeting as like having company over for a meal. We generally don't just plop the food on the table. First, we decide who we will invite and choose a date and time. We plan the menu, prepare the food, and set the table.

Guests arrive, and we welcome them and settle in. Then the meal happens, often in courses. After the meal, we clear the table, put away the leftovers, and wash the dishes. At some point, we say our goodbyes and our guests leave.

Meetings are the same — they have an energetic flow. No matter how long the meeting may be, the general arc of the agenda goes something like this:

- Beginning: Winding Up
  - Gathering.
  - Welcome and Opening.
  - Review the agenda (including the purpose, desired outcomes, and the processes you will use—the POP!).*
  - Meeting Guidelines.*
  - Check-in.*
- Middle: The Heart of the Meeting
  - Topics and issues to be considered with appropriate processes to meet the desired outcomes. It is helpful to note whether agenda items require a decision or input, or if people are just being informed about the topic.
- End: Winding Down
  - Next Steps and Follow-up.
  - Meeting Evaluation.*
  - Closing Check-out.

* See Tools and Resources

Here is a template for a facilitator's agenda, which includes all the detail the facilitator needs to lead the meeting.

**Name of Organization**
**Name of Meeting**

## Date and Time
## Location

## Facilitator's Agenda

**Facilitator:**

**Purpose:**

**Desired Outcomes:**

| TIME | ITEM | PROCESS to USE/QUESTIONS to ASK | MATERIALS/NEEDS |
|------|------|-------------------------------|-----------------|
|      |      |                               |                 |
|      |      |                               |                 |
|      |      |                               |                 |
|      |      |                               |                 |
|      |      |                               |                 |
|      |      |                               |                 |
|      |      |                               |                 |

From the facilitator's agenda, you can develop a participant agenda, which omits process details but may include times, depending on what you think is best for the group. The participant agenda can be sent out in advance.

## Name of Organization
## Name of Meeting

**Date and Time**
**Location**

**Participant Agenda**

**Facilitator:**

**Purpose:**

**Desired Outcomes:**

## Agenda

- Opening and Check-in
- Item 1
  - Key question that will guide the discussion
- Item 2
  - Key question that will guide the discussion
- Item 3
  - Key question that will guide the discussion
- Closing and Meeting Evaluation
- Next Steps

## Shifting the Plan

In order to truly meet people where they are and create the possibility of transformation, we need to be open to the possibility that meeting agendas may need to shift. Despite our best planning efforts, unanticipated things can emerge in meetings that genuinely do require attention. We need to know when and how to carefully and lovingly shift if that is what the group needs.

Some ideas that emerge in meetings — random thoughts, cool tangents — don't need attention. Sometimes these ideas may be attempts to avoid difficult conversations, especially if they come from people with strong personalities or positions. Knowing the interests and issues at play in a group helps me hold the process clearly and listen for when new topics or questions do require us to shift our plan.

Parking Lots are a great tool for dealing with new topics or emerging questions that aren't right for the current moment but that we want to hold onto and address later. They allow people to voice their ideas and then let go of them for the time being. For in-person meetings, the parking lot can be a sheet of paper hanging at the front of the room. For virtual meetings, we can designate a spot in a Docs or Google Slides, or we can ask people to put their ideas in the chat and the notetaker can record them. I've heard many fun and environmentally-minded names for this tool like the Bike Rack and the Bus Stop. A sustainable agriculture group called it the Hayloft and a sustainable fisheries group chose the Dock.

As time slips away, it's common for later agenda items to get lost. I try to use the perception of time scarcity as an asset, not to rush to agreement or coercion but to help people let go of whatever is keeping them stuck. It can be a delicate dance to strike this balance. Time scarcity can usher in urgency, which paves the way for flawed thinking, exclusion, and dominance. But held gently, like a tickling feather, it can help folks let go of superfluous things they are holding onto.

I learned a very useful phrase from Joyce Shabazz for when time is tight and people have a lot to say: "For the sake of time..." This beautiful phrase can gracefully move groups along (e.g., "For the sake of time, let's take just one more comment") helping people to relax and understand that we all share the responsibility for how we use our time together.

The larger the group, the more conservative I am about shifting agendas. If there are three people in a meeting, shifting the agenda is like steering a scooter — super easy. Twelve people are more like a sedan — a shift requires thought and intention and is harder to reverse. Larger groups are like tractor-trailers — it takes a lot of intention and care to make sure you're shifting in just the right direction while keeping everyone on board.

Small shifts — staying together as a whole group instead of breaking into trios, skipping an icebreaker or energizer because we extended a break — can be easily made by facilitators on the fly. But when the possibility of significant shifting emerges, I do at least two reality checks: first with myself and then with the group. Shifting the agenda means that we may not reach our intended outcomes. The group, particularly the people in leadership, must agree to that. If people are okay with letting go of outcomes, we need to figure out when and where we will address the things we are not getting to. Making sure everyone in the group is willing to change the agenda helps us stay in one conversation together.

When agendas and outcomes need to shift, they need to shift. Maybe something significant has happened and needs to be processed? Maybe a previously obscured truth has emerged? If the energy to shift the agenda is still strong and clear after I have reality tested, asked whether the new issue belongs in the parking lot and worked with the group to make mindful decisions about time and outcomes, it's time to do it.

We had an excellent plan for the space committee's second meeting — an evening call on Zoom. We developed an upbeat, creative agenda to spark innovation as the task group considered how In Loving Hands, a large arts organization, would allocate space in their new facility.

In our opening check-in, we learned that two group members, Maggie and Lara, had just experienced sad news in their personal lives. Others were exhausted and almost everyone was anxious and discouraged by the news of the day, a school shooting in the Midwest. A few people mentioned particular concerns about the organization's history with space allocation. It was clear that the agenda we had planned was not a fit for the moment.

I privately messaged Gemma, the executive director, about what to do. She wanted to hear about the concerns. I checked in with the group to ensure they were up for continuing the meeting, given what people were holding. "I'm hearing a lot of pain and exhaustion and people are holding a lot of worry," I said. "I want to check in and make sure that people are still up for meeting tonight." They agreed that they were.

I proposed that we hear more about the concerns about how space had been allocated in the past. We did a thumb poll to see if the group agreed (see Tools and Resources). Most people gave the proposal a thumbs up. Jojo and Barri had their thumbs sideways, which meant they had some concerns. They wanted to make sure the conversation considered how space would eventually be allocated. I shared that that had been my intention, and we all agreed to move forward.

We did two go-arounds in a circle process, hearing from each person twice (see Tools and Resources). During the second round, ideas for the space emerged and people were energized. By the time we ended our meeting, we had generated several creative and viable ideas. Not only had we reached our original desired outcome, but we had also cared for group members and attended to a key issue within the organization.

Regardless of whether an agenda shifts, it's important to leave appropriate time to end meetings well. I am physically incapable of leaving a meeting without clear next steps. My internal sensor activates because I know how critical follow-up and follow-through are. Many good ideas languish if nobody carries them forward.

It's important to confirm the decisions we have made as well as who has agreed to do what, and by when, to move the decisions forward. Taking the time to ensure a shared understanding of next steps and agreements fosters accountability and follow-through.

## Space

The spaces where we meet contribute significantly to the success of our meetings, both in person and virtually. The central questions around space are: *Where should we meet, and how can the space we meet in contribute to the quality of our work?*

I'm a big fan of going off site for meetings and retreats that require generative and creative thinking. I have facilitated meetings in dorm rooms, classrooms, board rooms, beautiful retreat centers in natural surroundings, and a few times in a World War II bunker. We don't need to pack up the car and drive two hours to the mountains for a weekly staff meeting. But being in a spacious, calming place outside our daily routine can greatly enhance creative visioning or deep problem solving. Environments that invite our bodies and spirits to be fully present open pathways for new thinking.

My friend and fellow consultant, Julia Riseman, says that a retreat location should be a statement of appreciation. People who attend a retreat are giving extra time and energy to their organization. Providing them with a space that holds them well shows respect, cares for them, and lets them know that their contributions are valued.

During the COVID-19 pandemic, I did not attend an in-person meeting for two years. I missed so much about being "in the room" with people: the energy, the physicality, the joy of companionship. And I missed the people who work in retreat and meeting facilities, where I have often appreciated a remarkable hospitality. I am always grateful when staff check in regularly to ensure the space is conducive to our activities and go out of their way to care for participants with food and other logistics. There are so many ways facility staff contribute to the container of off-site meetings. I encourage participants to appreciate these folks, including with generous tips.

Off-site locations must be culturally accessible for all participants. I've been invited to retreats and meetings at board members' homes that turned out to be actual mansions. For many people who do not have that level of resources, being in that kind of environment can inhibit participation.

Here are some things I've learned about making meeting spaces inviting and comfortable:

- Natural light is an essential factor for me. Without it, I find the quality of our presence and thinking diminishes.
- Sharing food is a great way to build connections and share a common human experience. Be sure to accommodate dietary restrictions.
- Our bodies need to be comfortable. We are more likely to keep our hearts and minds present and open for six

hours in comfortable chairs with space to move around than crammed together on hard wooden pews.

- I usually play music when people arrive and during breaks. In both virtual and in-person meetings, I use music as a cue to let people know that breaks are ending. When the music stops, it's time to come back — kind of like musical chairs!

- For in-person meetings, I make colorful posters and hang them on the walls to use as templates or cues (e.g., the agenda and parking lot). In virtual meetings, it can be helpful to use beautiful slides, interactive templates, and other technology to shape the space in different ways.

- I think better when I'm doodling or have something to do with my hands, so I like to have something for people to fidget with. Pipe cleaners, Play-Doh, and Model Magic are good listening aids that also lend themselves to creative expression. At some retreats, we've produced enough art to have a little showing at the end!

Along with the loss, grief, and reverberating suffering, the COVID-19 pandemic has offered us many lessons including learning about the power and limitations of virtual meetings.

We all know the frustrations: technical challenges; tiny boxes; constant opportunities for distraction; loss of relationship time during breaks, meals, and other in-between spaces; and the absence of the energy that builds when we are physically together.

However, there are also upsides: accessible meetings for folks with disabilities and other travel challenges; no travel time; lower (or no!) costs; and a different kind of intimacy that can emerge from the perceived safety of physical distance. For these reasons, I will continue to facilitate virtually when it best meets the needs of a group, or is the only option.

## Accessibility

For many years, I have facilitated an annual planning event for By All Means, a national advocacy group for people with disabilities. Each year we met at a beautiful hotel in the Bay Area. The hotel did an excellent job accommodating the needs of more than 25 participants with physical disabilities.

I went into the bathroom on a break during the last year we met at that hotel. I ran into Mary, one of the participants, waiting at the entrance. Mary rides in a wheelchair and there was a long line of empty stalls. She told me she was waiting for the accessible stall at the end of the row. When a non-accessible stall become available, I went in.

On my way out, I saw Mary still waiting for the accessible stall. "Is everything alright?" I asked.

"I've been waiting over five minutes, but the person isn't coming out," she replied.

I checked the accessible stall and discovered that there was nobody in it and it was locked! The next nearest accessible bathroom was on a different floor, but at that point it was Mary's only option. I held the break longer than expected to give her enough time, and we spoke with the facility's staff to ensure that never happened again.

I am learning that accessibility needs to be a mindset, not an afterthought. With the patience and guidance of clients, friends, and family members who are people with disabilities or advocates for people with disabilities, I am continuing to learn how to plan all meetings so that everyone present can participate to their fullest capacity. This goes well beyond physical needs.

The central question around accessibility is: *How can the logistics, space, and processes for this meeting work well for all participants?*

My friend Shaya French, a disability community organizer, generously crafted the recommendations below. Their words are calling me to expand my practices, and I am very grateful.

*We all have access needs. If a meeting were held on the 30th floor of a building without an elevator, that would be inaccessible for most people. However, some people's access needs are factored in from the start, and other people have to disclose and advocate for those needs.*

*It is important to plan for accessibility for a wide range of people from the beginning. If you know your community has particular accessibility needs, like a wheelchair accessible space or Spanish interpretation, start early to make sure you can find the right space and book an interpreter. It's also important to gather information from the people attending about what they need. Often this is done as part of registration and should include the contact info of whom to contact about accessibility requests before and during the event. One mistake I often see folks making is not even providing people with the information they need to know if they will have trouble accessing a space.*

*Here's a non-comprehensive list:*

- *What is the accessibility of the physical space (e.g., wheelchair-accessible bathrooms, steps, size inclusivity of the chairs, distance from public transit, parking options, etc.)?*
- *Will we be sitting in chairs or on the floor?*
- *Are there breaks?*
- *Will there be small groups all talking in a room at the same time?*
- *Will people have to stand for a long time?*
- *Are there visual images like a PowerPoint?*
- *Are we eating food together? What dietary options are already provided?*

- *Will CART (captions provided in real time by a person) or ASL (American Sign Language) interpretation be provided automatically or only upon request?*
- *How will people be asked to participate? Will participants have to write anything?*

*A helpful way to come up with things you should inform people about is to ask yourself if the event will include anything unusual that people might not expect, like an icebreaker that requires physical movement or touching other people.*

*An additional way to make a space work for everyone is to ask people to share their access needs in the introduction go-round. It is helpful to go through the schedule before asking about any access needs, keeping in mind the list of examples above to highlight places where there might need to be modifications. To introduce the idea of access needs, I often say a few sentences about what they are and then give a few examples, such as "I need everyone to speak up so I can hear." or "My child is with a babysitter so I need to keep my phone on and may need to step out to take a phone call if anything comes up." It's helpful to show that access needs are not only about disability. I encourage people who don't have access needs at that moment to say, "My access needs are being met by this space." Following accessibility practices can make the difference between your event feel welcoming and inclusive to participants versus alienating and upsetting.*

As we create containers for meetings, we must pay attention so we don't recreate the disrespect and assaults to dignity that people with disabilities and language accessibility needs often experience.

## Attending to Equity

As much as I can, in every moment, I am working to not collude with racism and other forms of oppression. Through the limits of my human filter, my whiteness, and other aspects of my identity, I strive to stay attuned to ensuring equity of voice while watching for and undoing oppressive dynamics in ways that invite connection and curiosity.

I interrupt when I hear potentially harmful or oppressive comments. This is not neutral. I do it with simple redirection, without humiliation or shame.

I watched the words tumble out of Victor's mouth in slow motion and saw the immediate hurt and disbelief on his colleague's faces, particularly his colleagues who were Black and other people of color. It was a staff meeting about hiring practices. Victor, a white man, had voiced what some white people sometimes erroneously think: "If we prioritize hiring people of color, we'll be lowering the quality of applicants and our staff."

I listened only long enough to be sure I understood what he was saying and then interrupted and addressed him directly: "Victor, I know that's something that white people sometimes think, but this isn't true at all." Matter of fact and clear. I took a breath, looked around, to see if anyone needed to say anything more to be complete in that moment, Nobody did, and we moved on.

Here are some practices and techniques that I have found helpful for creating and maintaining spaces that honor human identities and equity of voice:

- Welcoming everyone into the space as they arrive, with particular attention to people from historically marginalized identities.

- Notice who is speaking and who isn't. Rather than calling on the first hands that spring up, ask people who have already talked to wait if others haven't yet had a chance. I invite people who haven't spoken much to speak. Depending on the context, I may reach out to individuals by name or just put the invitation to the group. I try to avoid anything that could be at all humiliating. All these years later, I still feel the sting of being randomly called on in middle school and not knowing the answer!
- Gently (at first) interrupt when people are speaking over each other or going on too long.
- Avoid processes that prioritize extroverts and people from dominant identities.
- Ask clear questions about the topic and go around the room to hear everyone's response.
- Break up into pairs or small groups to consider a question and then report back to the whole group. This can be helpful in a few different ways. Small groups and pairs have an intimacy that larger groups lack. The format can build comfort for shyer or newer people and foster relationships between participants. It can also disrupt emerging dominant behaviors. It is important to give the groups clear directions. Let them know how much time they have and what will be expected of them when everyone comes back together. It can also be helpful to remind people to practice listening to each other with care, especially if that is part of the Meeting Guidelines.
- Silent drawing, individual writing, and reflection are good ways to slow down and let people connect with their own thinking. This technique can be particularly helpful for introverts.

My daughter Zoe taught me a helpful distinction between different types of processing: microwave and crockpot thinkers.

Microwave thinkers come up with their responses right away. They may or may not be on track, but they're ready to answer questions almost as soon as they are posed. Crockpot thinkers need time to stew on an idea before they are ready to say what they think. They often give insightful answers but need time to process. As a microwave thinker, I must remember to ask myself what all kinds of thinkers need. What questions will people need in advance? What kind of time and space for reflection might be useful? I've also had to learn to take a few breaths after someone has stopped speaking and ask them if they are complete before moving on.

I often explain to groups why we are doing what we are doing. I want to spread the use of practices that support equity and shift power and I love hearing that people are using processes they learned from our work together.

## Decision-Making

*We are always only one bad decision away from inequity.*
— Felicia Sullivan

*Should we enter into this new partnership? How much time should we expect people to spend in the office? Should we expand a program?* Organizations decide things all the time. Large and (seemingly) small decisions determine how we manifest our aspirations and spend our time and resources. We make some decisions individually and some in groups, some mindfully and some without much conscious thought. We make many (though by no means all) of our organizational decisions in meetings.

Organizational decision-making matters not only because it shapes how things get done but because it reveals how power operates — who influences and controls what will happen, now and in the future. As I work with clients, it's important for me to understand how decision-making is living in their system. Is

171

it clear? Is it consistent? Is it appropriately inclusive? Unclear and mis-aligned decision-making processes are at the root of a lot of organizational dysfunction, mistrust, and relationship challenges. Regardless of the work we are doing together, my consulting engagements often involve decision-making. One way I address this topic is by providing opportunities for my clients to build toward values-aligned, equitable, clear decision-making.

Some common problematic decision-making patterns that I watch out for, both in meetings and throughout an organization, include:

- Unclear process — not clearly defining the process, including when the decision will be made, how it will be made, and who will make it (including distinguishing between who will have input at specific stages and who will make the final decision)
- Lack of transparency — not sharing the process with the people who will be involved and/or affected
- Hasty decision-making — making decisions before all the relevant information has been gathered and considered
- Lack of inclusion — making decisions lacking key voices and perspectives, which may mean that they don't meet the needs or further the liberation of stakeholders
- Over-inclusion — including people in decision-making processes who do not have a vested stake in the outcome or relevant wisdom to share, which often happens when there is mistrust or fear of making unpopular decisions
- Too much process — drawn-out processes, especially for relatively small or unimportant issues
- Decision-making by default — not attending to decisions mindfully or in timely ways

If we dig deeper, we often find that the underlying problem is how decisions about decision-making are made. An important step toward shifting power in organizations — and the world — is clarifying decision-making processes and centering them as much as possible around the people closest to and most impacted by what is being decided. When organizations, even progressive ones, are not mindful about how they make decisions, they tend to fall back on ways of decision-making that keep power in the hands of those with dominant identities and/or positional power.

"I'm not sure how it happened," Simon told me, his voice tinged with fear and regret. He was a white man, the executive director of Muddy Shoes (a children's museum and creative space), and a long-time client. He had called me for some coaching to help him think through a dilemma.

He continued, "As you know, our agreement is that the management team makes decisions about management-level hiring and promotions by consensus. When Felicity, our program director, gave notice, I wanted to promote Sylvie from program manager into the role. You know how great she is and what a stellar job she does. I thought it was a no brainer.

In our weekly management team meeting last week I suggested Sylvie's promotion and everyone agreed. After the meeting I offered Sylvie the job and was so glad when she accepted! Then I sent an email to the board and staff announcing her promotion. Wow, was I surprised. Wanda and Chris came running into my office. They claimed they never agreed to the promotion, and they were pissed. But they were in the meeting! I reminded them that we had all agreed and they claimed that's not what happened. I just don't understand!"

I wanted to learn more about what had caused this misunderstanding. "Tell me what you said and what questions you asked when you thought you were reaching agreement," I said.

"Well, I told everyone what the proposal was — that Sylvie would be promoted to program director and join the management team. I asked if that was okay with everyone, and nobody said no, so I thought we were good to go."

"That sounds confusing," I said, affirming his emotional response. "It's so great that you've got a structure where the whole management team makes these decisions together — you all have a strong commitment to sharing power. But in order to really do that, you need to put careful attention toward how you make decisions." I pointed out that he had assumed a lack of response meant agreement. A very common mistake.

"Shit" he said, "that is exactly what I did. I was so excited about the idea that I just assumed everyone would love it."

"What else might you, or others in the group, have done differently?" I asked.

He thought for a moment. "I really don't know," he mused.

"Let's think about the steps we've talked about to reach agreements as a group," I suggested.

"Oh, yeah," Simon said, shaking his head. "I really didn't give them time to think about the proposal in advance, and I definitely didn't ask if anyone had any concerns or questions, and I was not careful to make sure they all agreed."

"You were really excited about the idea, and strong feelings can sometimes lead us away from what we know to be good process," I said. "Do you have other thoughts about what else could have been different?"

"Well, I do wish people had spoken up. Why didn't they say anything in the meeting?"

"You're white, and Wanda and Chris are Black. You're the ED and have the most positional power. I'm thinking that dynamics of race and power are present here," I said.

Simon thought for a moment. "Yeah, as the person with more positional power, as a white man, I really messed up — I wasn't thinking about that — I was assuming that the trust we had built up was enough. I just moved forward how I wanted to move."

Simon was committed to doing what he needed to do to repair the situation. He understood that his position and identity gave him power that he needed to continually examine, including finding support to unpack his actions and impulses. It was easy for him to forget that people could default to his wishes and be reluctant to tell him the truth.

As we spoke, Simon developed a plan to return to the management team and acknowledge fully his mistake and open a conversation about the process, future decision-making, and how to move forward.

There are many tools and processes that help groups come to wise agreements in just ways. The Tools and Resources section in the back of this book includes some of them, such as Circle Processes and Deep Democracy. Fundamental to all these processes is helping people listen deeply to each other, speak their truths, and create enough trust to hold the well-being of the whole alongside, or even ahead of, their own personal interest.

When a decision has to be made, the people who are ultimately in charge of the decision (an executive director, a board, a management team) need to clarify who will:

- Make the decision, either as an individual or a group
- Weigh in on the issue but not make the actual decision Their input will inform the decision-makers, who can choose how to use their input and advice
- Be informed about the decision but have no input

I ask the following key questions to help leaders think about who should be included and in what capacity:

- Who will be impacted by this decision?
- Who has wisdom to contribute to this decision (i.e., important knowledge about the topic, context, or dynamic)?
- Whose investment and support is critical to successful implementation of this decision?

Interaction Institute for Social Change talks about "Maximum Appropriate Involvement" in decision-making. Different decisions require different levels of inclusion, and the goal is to involve the right people in the right ways.

A client once told me of an organization-wide committee that had met for nine months to decide on a color to paint their lobby. It was frustrating and time consuming, and half the people still didn't like the end result! The process frayed trust and left people reluctant to sign up for committees.

A decision-making body (e.g., a board, staff team, committee, neighborhood council) needs:

- A clear understanding of the decision-making process before they get started
- Time to build an understanding of the issues at hand
- Effective processes for listening and deliberating
- Willingness to engage in continued inquiry, deep listening, and truth telling

I work with my clients to design meeting processes that help people achieve understanding, develop and refine plans, and reach agreements in ways that support human connection and align with their values. I can think of only a few times when groups I worked with insisted on making a decision by majority vote. Voting, by definition, sets up winners and losers, which does not help build alignment within groups. I prefer to facilitate processes that result in agreements that everyone involved can support. Though consensus can have a bad reputation, seeking consensus is at the heart of these processes.

Consensus doesn't mean that everyone gets their first choice or that we have compromised until the decision is a shadow of what it might have been. It means that we have listened deeply enough that everyone can be on board with our chosen direction. I think about consensus as reaching agreements that can be greater than the sum of their parts, made stronger by deep understanding.

Here are the steps I use to facilitate groups to reach agreements:

1. Clarify the decision to be made:
   ◦ What are the issues at stake?
   ◦ Why now?
   ◦ What context or background information will people need to make a good decision?

2. Clarify the process by which the decision will be made:
   - Who will be involved and in what capacity?
   - Who is the final decision maker?
   - If we are seeking agreement in this group, how will we achieve that?
   - What is the timeline and how much time is available?
   - What will we do if we can't reach agreement in the time allotted?
3. Develop or present a proposal for the group to decide on:
   - A smaller group or an individual can develop a proposal beforehand and bring it to the larger group for consideration.
   - Groups can also develop proposals as part of the process.
4. Clarify and refine the proposal as needed:
   - It's critical for everyone involved in making the decision to understand the proposal and have the opportunity to surface their questions and concerns.
   - As groups strive for understanding, they need time and space for reflection and dialogue.
   - These conversations may result in revisions to the proposal, which in turn need to be understood and, ultimately, accepted by the entire group.
5. Look for agreement or identify divergence:
   - Ask for verbal agreement or a show of hands; or do a Thumb Poll (see Tools and Resources).
   - If there is agreement, clearly state that a decision has been made and name or describe the decision to ensure that everyone agrees.
   - If the group is not in agreement, clearly name the areas of divergence. Again, the Deep Democracy question "What do you need to come along?" is very useful in surfacing concerns and amending proposals until agreement can be reached.

- ○ In some cases, people may choose to stand aside from a decision or even remove themselves from a group if they are not in agreement with the direction the rest of the group is choosing.
6. Follow up:
   - ○ Verbally and/or in writing, confirm the decision and identify the next steps (who will do what by when).
   - ○ Notify everyone affected by the decision!

If we want to engage in just decision-making, we must purposefully build organizational cultures and processes that create enough safety for people to engage in processes that share power and which allow each member of a group to be heard and to reach their own conclusions. This is particularly true across race and other dimensions of difference. People need to know and trust that there are predictable processes for inclusion and that their participation will be treated with care.

# Facilitating: Holding Space

*My job as a facilitator is to use my power to meet people's needs, and then make a series of effective interventions that help them take a series of cascading risks to love each other a little bit more deeply than before.*

— Megan Pamela Ruth Madison

*Love is more than a feeling. Love is a form of sweet labor. Fierce, bloody, imperfect and lifegiving. A choice we make over and over again. If love is sweet labor, love can be taught, modeled and practiced.*

— Valarie Kaur

As a consultant, I spend most of my time holding space for others to think, dream, explore, and plan. I facilitate processes for people to sit more fully with what is true, challenge old stories and limiting beliefs, lean into love, and allow new ideas and plans to emerge. Although I do a fair amount of individual leadership coaching as part of organizational interventions, most of my work is with groups.

I sometimes imagine facilitating as orchestra conducting. I am exquisitely attuned to what is happening. Everything outside the space disappears; there's nothing but the people I am with. I am listening with attention rooted in my body. What's underneath the words? What's not being said? Whose voices are we hearing, and whose are we not? What clarity is emerging?

I am not making music, but my movements are subtly designed to bring forth brilliance and music that is in a state of potentiality.

Facilitate literally means to make things easier. Well-planned and skillfully facilitated meetings can be a joy. That's not just me speaking as a process nerd; it is what I often hear from clients. I treasure my role as a facilitator, making things easy for groups to listen, talk, discern, love, create new ideas, deepen understanding, and move together through difficult places.

Though people use the word facilitation for both, I see a difference between leading workshops or training and facilitating organizational development processes. I think of training as helping individuals learn a body of content or skills, while process facilitation is about helping a group of people journey to someplace new together. Training may be collaborative and interactive and can be a component of organizational development interventions. Process facilitation may also include building content knowledge and developing skills. With training, however, the trainer is generally the center of the action. Process facilitation centers the group, even when the facilitator stands in front of the room.

That said, both facilitative trainers and process facilitators co-create and maintain stable containers for connection and interaction. They create a sense of belonging and care that allows people to hear and experience each other and themselves in new and deeper ways.

I once heard a facilitator interviewed on a podcast. They spoke of coming into facilitation because they loved to be the center of attention. My skin crawled when I heard that. No, I thought, facilitation is the opposite of being about us! It's about using our full selves to bring something new into the world, about making space for the ideas and awareness hidden in each of us to ignite and shine. Fortunately, the facilitator went on to say they had learned that facilitation is exactly the opposite of being the center of attention. Phew!

For me, the posture of facilitation is humility. I learned a beautiful phrase about humility from the wise writing of

Rabbi Alan Morinis when I was studying the Jewish spiritual practice of Mussar with Rabbi David Jaffe: "No more than my space, no less than my place." This precisely captures how I think about my role — taking up just the right amount of space so that people can shine brilliantly, no more, no less. When I'm facilitating, I sometimes repeat this phrase to myself as a reminder.

Though I wasn't aware of it at the time, I can see now that I became a facilitator because I so often felt uncomfortable in groups. What were the rules? When was my voice welcome? How vulnerable could or should I be? Could someone stop so many men from taking up so much space?! I sometimes felt, and can still feel, silenced and awkward in groups, particularly if they are unskillfully facilitated. I want to be in spaces of belonging, care, and authenticity. Amidst all our human messiness, facilitation gives us tools to be in the same conversations as each other at the same time, to deepen our understanding, and, ideally, to rise to our better angels together.

When done well, process facilitation can barely be seen. But it takes art, skill, patience, and a fair amount of science to achieve that sense of a meeting unfolding organically! This chapter explores some elements of facilitating processes that make the seemingly magical happen: building trust, asking questions and listening, reflecting and synthesizing, showing up with presence and vulnerability, sharing our own stories, and committing to our own growth and development.

Like any kind of authentic leadership, facilitation is a way of being rather than a check-list of dos and don'ts. There are many books and training resources about facilitation methods (I have included some of my favorites in Tools and Resources), but you won't find much here about specific activities and techniques. Rather, this chapter is about what it means to BE a facilitator.

## Trust

"Moving at the speed of trust" is a phrase I first read in Stephen Covey's work. And it's true! Our work to bring about justice and love only moves as fast as our trust in our colleagues, comrades, and collaborators. Trust builds through relationships as we follow up and follow through on our word, hold confidences, and show up authentically and congruently with our values.

Trust is hard won and can be easily broken. It must be tended with care. I think of it as a kind of energy. When cultivated well and mindfully, it gives life and power to whatever people do together.

As I work with clients, I am often a bridge of trust, lending my sense of trust for others to travel across. I bring faith in myself and trust that, with the right processes and support, this group of humans can figure out what they need to figure out. When met with trust and held with care, most people can eventually rise above hurts and personal interests to touch their place of love and find common good.

Some ways to build trust in groups include:

- Taking time to hear each other's stories
- Providing opportunities for 1:1 conversations so people can get to know each other outside of typical meeting interactions
- Demonstrating trust in individuals and the group
- Demonstrating belief in the fundamental capacity of the group to do what they need to do
- Welcoming authentic truths when they are spoken
- Including processes that attend to continual relationship-building
- Taking enough time for people to be able to really see and hear each other
- Welcoming all questions

Racism, sexism, and other forms of oppression are inherent barriers to trust. When I walk into a room, my identity comes with me. I am likely up against some sexism, perhaps antisemitism, ageism, heightism, etc. It is important that I notice these things when they are present and not take them personally. When people perpetuate dominance and oppression, I must hold them accountable for their behaviors while not losing trust in their fundamental humanity. This takes practice and deep inner grounding.

I am glad to see the common myth of the neutral facilitator slowly disappearing. As a facilitator, I am in service to everyone in the room; I do not advocate for or support any particular position. And yet, I am rarely neutral. I don't usually have a particular opinion about whether my client chooses option A or option B, but I do have a very clear set of values that guide me. These include dignity, justice, love, integrity, liberation, and compassion. On these, I am not neutral. It is my goal to stand for these values everywhere I go.

Instead of neutrality, I prefer a term I learned from Deep Democracy: equanimity, meaning stability and composure. Operating from a place of equanimity requires me to manage my own issues when they emerge as I care for everyone's voice. It means holding the space of dignity for all while still standing clear in my values. Holding people with equanimity, as their best possible selves, makes possible the broader vision and trust that is essential for transformation.

### Essential Facilitation Skills: Listening, Asking Questions, Reflecting, and Synthesizing

*To listen fully means to pay close attention to what is being said beneath the words. You listen not only to the "music," but to the essence of the person speaking. You listen not only for what someone knows, but for what he or she is. Ears operate at the speed of sound, which is far slower than the speed of light the eyes*

*take in. Generative listening is the art of developing*
*deeper silences in yourself, so you can slow your mind's*
*hearing to your ears' natural speed and hear beneath the*
*words to their meaning.*

— Peter Senge

As I mentioned earlier, Barry Oshry describes facilitators as "designated listeners." We listen with careful attention, and we often reflect back to people what we are hearing them say. Our skilled listening creates an opening for people to lend their attention to others and hear themselves in new ways.

I have been blessed to have many good and generous listeners in my life. When I talk with someone who knows how to listen, my faith in my own wisdom grows. I can hear thoughts and ideas come out of my mouth that I didn't even know I had. As Carol Gilligan has said, "We are listened into being."

I noticed some years back that my listening has a volume control. Without being aware of what I was doing, I was turning it up or down depending on my interest level. Now I continually strive to raise the volume of my listening attention, especially when facilitating a group or supporting an individual to connect more deeply with their own thinking.

I grew up in New York Jewish culture where interrupting is a way of life. As my friend Kathryn says, it's how we let each other know we're paying attention. But interrupting can land as rude and disrespectful for folks outside that culture. I try to notice my urge to interrupt and discern if it will be helpful, or if I need to listen longer and breathe to calm my nervous system.

Some helpful guidelines for generative listening that helps people connect with their own thinking are:

- Pay attention! If you feel your mind wandering, bring your attention back to the present moment with your breath. Remember that a precious human soul is saying something important to them.

- Don't fake your understanding. Tell the truth when you don't understand. Ask for clarifying details if you need them. If you, the facilitator, are not understanding something, it's almost certain that others in the group are also confused.
- Do not imagine you know what the speaker will say or how they feel. Suspend your temptation to draw conclusions and finish others' sentences.
- Remember your intention. What quality of presence do you want to bring to your listening, and what experience would you like the speaker to have?

I have learned to stay longer in silence than is comfortably the norm. This can be hard to do. Often, my first impulse is to break silence to help move the conversation along. But I know that taking time is important. I breathe into my faith that a group can choose to let their brilliance emerge. This creates space to call forth a deeper level of presence in the group. Even when it's uncomfortable, we can use the experience of being in silence together to learn about what it means for us to work and be together.

I use the spice of advocacy judiciously. I speak up if I hear my clients heading toward a decision that I believe is inconsistent with their values and goals or that I strongly suspect, based on my experience, will not go well. Or when I hear groupthink taking over: people abdicating their critical thinking and ideas under the persuasion of powerful voices.

My interventions are usually well received, as most of my clients understand that I am there to help them reach their intended outcomes. And sometimes it's received as a pain in the ass, thank you very much.

Asking powerful and true questions is another crucial facilitative tool. Here are some guidelines for asking questions that invite people into a deeper well of thinking:

- Ask only real questions, not questions where you already know the answer.
- Ask open-ended questions that do not have yes or no answers. These kinds of questions keep people talking so they can hear themselves think.
- Ask only questions for which you are willing to hear an answer.
- If "you asshole" fits easily at the end of a question, it's good to either rephrase, check your tone, or hold the question altogether.

When we want to ask a question, we must ask ourselves why. Joyce Shabazz asks herself, "Is it only to satisfy my own curiosity?" If so, then it is not the question for the facilitating moment. But if you want to help someone enter a place of discovery for themselves, ask away!

A phrase I've heard so many times is often said in one rapid breath: *"Everybody good with that? Great, let's move on."* Just writing it causes my insides to contract. *Wait, you asked...I didn't have a moment to think, and then boom, my voice didn't matter anyway.* It is energetically jarring and alienating when we ask people questions that aren't really questions.

When I ask a question, I need to truly take time to hear the answer. If I ask a question that raises an issue a group is unprepared for, I need to figure out what to do with it right then and there. Will we deal with it in the moment? Should we put it in a Parking Lot? When we don't honor real answers to questions we've asked, we undermine the group's confidence and trust. Before I ask a question, I need to ask myself if I am prepared to hear what might emerge. Do we have the time and space? Is the system or group ready?

Questions have thresholds. For example, if a small group brings a proposal to a larger group, they need to be clear about what they are looking for. Are they open to all feedback and changes? This is a low threshold. Nobody needs to jump very high to join the conversation. If they only want to hear about serious objections or things people can't live with, they need to ask a high-threshold question that will preempt wordsmithing and comments about small details.

A third facilitative skill is reflecting back what people have said. I paraphrase what people say and check that I have heard them correctly. This kind of reflecting holds up a mirror so people can hear themselves and others can listen to them more deeply. It can foster greater understanding and new insights, even for the person whose words I am reflecting. I often see relief and visible relaxation as people understand that they have been heard — or have the opportunity to clarify what they meant if I have misunderstood or misrepresented them. I don't do this for every comment, but here are a few reasons I do it:

- If I sense that others are not paying full attention to the speaker
- If I sense that the statement might have been confusing for people
- If I sense that the person speaking may have more thinking that needs to be surfaced
- If someone makes a critically important point that I want to underscore and make sure everyone has understood

A fourth important facilitative skill is synthesizing. Facilitators look for patterns and themes; we surface areas of convergence and divergence and highlight new ideas as they emerge. We are the "designated noticer." We notice what is happening for the group without judgment, simply saying what we see. We test what we hear to see if it resonates. Again, it is not about getting it right; it's about helping the group members hear themselves and each other more deeply. I need always to be willing to hear someone or even the entire group say "No, that's not it!" and then, without defensiveness, listen again so I can be more accurate.

Often, I pull forward emerging ideas that are just taking shape. This can be tricky, as groups need to be ready to receive the ideas. I have found it effective to offer my synthesis as a guess rather than a proposition: "Here is what I'm hearing. How does that land for you?"

I believe that everyone can build these four essential skills to use both in meetings and as human beings contributing to more just communities and families.

## Presence and Vulnerability

While thoughtful processes and nifty techniques are important, presence and care are the most critical ingredients of meaningful facilitation. Our faith and confidence in the innate wisdom within individuals and groups makes the energetic space where inspiration and courage emerge.

Bringing our full presence to the people we are with invites them to let down their defenses and be present themselves. Our ability to be vulnerable, undefended, and connected with what is happening inside us enables us to build trust and connect with people authentically.

Several years ago, I participated in a workshop led by a very well-known and highly experienced consultant.

People had flown from all over the country to attend. On the second day, we gathered at 8:30 a.m. for breakfast and schmoozing before the workshop was to begin at 9.00 a.m. The workshop leader wasn't there. I was a little surprised, as I knew that connecting with participants was important to them. When they weren't there at 9.00 a.m., people began to worry. Calls and texts went unanswered.

One of my recurring anxiety dreams unfolded before my eyes: not being where I was supposed to be for a high-stakes meeting! My worry meter was dinging. Surely something terrible had happened!

Someone ran to the consultant's hotel. It turned out that their alarm had not gone off and they had overslept. Because they were traveling, they had taken a sleeping pill the night before. It was well after 10.00 a.m. when they arrived, and the workshop began.

I worried. This person was a model in the field! What would they do? How would they manage the shame I was sure they were experiencing? How would this impact the workshop?

What they did taught me a lot: they arrived unharried and matter-of-factly told the story of what had happened. They apologized, asked if anyone had anything they needed to say (nobody did), and began the workshop. They never mentioned it again. It blew my mind! I imagined myself living in shame for the rest of my life if that ever happened to me.

I received a powerfully modeled gift that day. I saw in real time the graceful possibility of being present with the impact of my own actions without getting stuck in an emotional response that could take my attention out of the present moment.

I have since had many opportunities to notice I have made a mistake, attend to its impact, and practice not getting stuck. Learning to make mistakes, not get stuck in shame, and not look for reassurance or absolution from the group, even subtly, has been very powerful for me.

Presence and vulnerability require a necessary ballast: an acute awareness that we are facilitating a space for the participants to grow. I believe it is inappropriate for facilitators to look to the groups we are working with to take care of our emotional well-being. I know not everyone agrees. But let me state my case. I believe it is our job to hold the group. I am often transformed myself as I work with clients, shedding fears and old ideas and coming more into presence. But when I am facilitating it is not the place for me to sort through my hurts and confusions. I need to tend to my own unhealed places on my own time. I believe it's about consent. What did we all sign up for when we entered the room? Surely not to caretake the emotional needs of the person who is supposed to be holding us!

It's a similar delicate balance when we use stories from our own lives and experiences. These can be helpful spices to open new ideas and build connections. But it can also be tricky. I learned a valuable guideline years ago as a youth worker: *for the sake of whom*? If I want to share a story about myself, I ask myself why. Why do I want to share this? Will it be a contribution to the group? Might it further their thinking and learning? Might it help them to connect with and trust me? If the answer to any of these questions is yes, it's my delight to share. But might I be seeking to boost my ego? To heal myself? If I answer yes to these questions, I breathe deeply and let the impulse to share pass.

"But bad things are always happening!" Jasmine, a Vietnamese-American woman, said. The management team sat comfortably in a circle, sipping delicious tea and coffee. As a cross-race consulting team, my colleague and I were leading a two-day team development retreat for one of our clients. It was the morning of the second day. The bright and cheerful room overlooked a stunning mountain view. We were talking about the impact of trauma and how it was showing up among their team. Such conversations can make us feel as if the traumatic events are happening at that very moment, prompting responses that do not always serve our own or the group's interests.

"Yes, that is true," I said in response to Jasmine, keenly aware of the many layers of personal, racialized, and inter-generational trauma in this multi-racial group. "Even as we are here with each other in this beautiful place, harmful things are happening in the world. And hurtful things have happened to each of us. The opportunity is to learn to tell the difference between what is happening now and what isn't. As we work inside ourselves to learn to tell the difference, we can create more space around past traumatic events so that when they come into our awareness, we have a choice over how to respond. It's hard work, but we can learn not to let overwhelming past events control us in the present."

I then shared the story of how three of my four grandparents came to the US from Eastern Europe during the pogroms (organized massacres) against Jews before the Holocaust and the impact that has had on me.

"My maternal grandmother, Bertha, and her sisters fled their small town in Poland in the middle of the night in the back of a haycart. They hid in a relative's apartment in

Warsaw for years until, one by one, as teenagers, they came by boat to the US. The rest of their relatives did not make it out and perished in Auschwitz, the Nazi concentration camp. I am named after my grandmother's cousin, who died there.

My grandmother, whom I loved dearly, visibly carried this trauma. She wouldn't let me out of her sight when I was a child. She was always looking to protect us from evil. Despite her love and care, I hold a great deal of intergenerational trauma that was passed on outside of anyone's conscious awareness. I learned to be alert, cautious, hyper-vigilant, and always looking for danger. I moved through the world with a strong need to control my environment. Before I began working to heal this trauma, my nervous system could go from zero to holocaust in the blink of an eye with the slightest whiff of a threat.

I have become increasingly aware of this pattern through leadership training, the study of trauma, coaching, and therapy. I have worked hard to become aware of when I am activated. And I continue to learn techniques to calm my nervous system and distinguish what is happening in the moment from my visceral experience of the past.

Antisemitism is indeed a real threat, and it is also true that most situations I am in do not hold that threat to my safety. Living in a hyper-vigilant state did not protect me from antisemitic threats, but rather kept me from being fully present and choosing how to respond to possible threats to my safety. These unhealed responses kept me from being my most powerful, compassionate self. And my self-healing journey continues as a critical piece of my consultant practice."

Jasmine and the others took a deep breath. I felt an even closer connection with everyone in the group as they listened to my story with care. My vulnerability in sharing this story allowed others from various backgrounds, including fellow Jews, to see the possibility that they could shift the responses conditioned by past traumas. My vulnerability in this trusted environment opened new possibilities because I could share a personal part of myself while staying grounded and present — and not requiring rescue or emotional care from the group.

As facilitators, it is ongoing and lifelong work to attend to healing the places in ourselves that keep us from being fully present and human with one another. It's deep work that we need to do to support justice, but we need to do it when we are not holding space for others.

## Who Facilitates?

I believe any meeting can benefit from skilled facilitation, but whether you need (or want) someone from outside the system to facilitate depends on what the process requires. An outside facilitator can bring equanimity, and the freedom for participants not to have to worry about the process. As Ron Heifetz says, you can't be on the dance floor and the balcony at the same time. However, it isn't always what's needed.

Questions I ask my clients when we are considering who should facilitate a process or meeting include:

- Will an outside facilitator create the container for honest conversations?

- Might someone from outside help people see things they might currently be missing?
- Does the situation require a high level of facilitation skill (e.g., the group is facing a complex challenge or has a lot of conflict)?
- Will an outside facilitator make it easier for people within the system to participate fully?
- Is the meeting sufficiently high stakes that it is worth putting resources toward bringing someone in?
- Will having an internal facilitator empower leadership and confidence within the organization?
- Will having someone who knows the situation intimately be beneficial?
- Is it logistically feasible — or necessary — to have someone from inside facilitate?

I love seeing people inside organizations build facilitation skills and capacity as a result of our engagement. I have clients who have seriously invested in building facilitation skills. It is a game changer when organizations consistently have meaningful, productive meetings and their staff know how to participate well. It saves time, supports effective work, builds relationships, and adds to workplace enjoyment. It also saves resources as over time they can rely less on outside consultants. Most gratifyingly, several people at organizations where I have consulted over the years have gone on to become consultants themselves, and some are now my treasured colleagues!

## The Inside Job
*Your spiritual practice will give you many gifts but don't expect it to relieve you of your human nature.*
— Alan Morinis

I have a life-long commitment to continually cultivating the trustworthiness and integrity that are fundamental to my work of fostering justice and nurturing love. As a living human and a recovering perfectionist, it takes ongoing attention and intention for me not to fall into more contracted and fearful ways of being. I am always tending my inner resources and personal healing in order to hold space for others authentically.

As I've already explored, what we bring energetically into "the room" with clients becomes part of what is present and informs what can happen when we work together. I am committed to showing up with love and care as best as I can, no matter what other human thoughts or experiences I have that day.

Even after many years of self-work, I can still get triggered by my clients' dilemmas or when processes go in unexpected directions. When my ego gets involved, I can lose connection with clarity and equanimity, worry that I'm not doing a good enough job, or bring the energy of my fear and conditioned dominance into a meeting. If my ego begins to take over, I can find myself in a kind of FOG that subtly influences the energy of an engagement or meeting.

As I've learned, FOG can stand for "Fucking Opportunity for Growth" or what my wise cousin and fellow consultant, Paul Behrman, calls "A spiritual challenge disguised as a work challenge." Practicing mindfulness helps me attend to my energy and the places where my ego wants to take center stage. I have a set of practices I do nearly every morning, including relatively modest amounts of sitting meditation, yoga, and often aerobic activity. I strive to start my day with my nervous system in a regulated place, no matter what is going on.

I have a few additional ways I attend to aligning with groups and containing my energy. The first I learned from my colleague Jay Vogt. Just before the start of any session, I excuse myself, find a quiet place (often the bathroom), close my eyes, breathe deeply, and call forth my highest and best self, the highest and best self of my co-facilitator if I have one, the highest and best self of the group, and lastly the highest and best self of the place where we are meeting and/or the organization sponsoring the work (this can include Zoom itself!). I imagine aligning these parts and I commit that the work we will do together will be in the service of justice and love. I also draw an "Angel Card" for each session. These beautiful little cards have single words with qualities like "trust," "truth," and "beauty" on them. I hold the quality that I draw with me during the meeting.

If possible, I keep a candle lit during meetings (this is much easier to do in virtual meetings). I also drink a lot of water when I am facilitating, more than usual. Keeping our bodies well-hydrated is vital for our good health. But there's another reason I do it. I imagine energy moving through the group and out into the world. By drinking a lot of water, I am moving energy in my body and not allowing it to get stuck.

Focus phrases, which I originally learned from Robert Gass, are another ongoing practice I use to attend to my energy and align with the energies of the people I am working with. I choose a phrase to repeat silently to myself before any significant act of leadership. These can range from sending an email or having a phone call to facilitating a multi-day retreat — it's all significant. The phrases I use reflect my purpose in some way. They call me back to my center, reground me, and clear me of any thoughts that might counter my purpose at that moment.

I close my eyes, breathe deeply, and connect with my focus phrase many times each day. I sometimes even do this visibly when I'm at the front of the room or on Zoom. It takes less than five seconds, and it is always powerful. I feel my energy clear and shift — to my higher and best self, who I want to be, and what I want to bring in every moment I am working or interacting with another human being.

It is important to find phrases that resonate and hold power for you. I change phrases as I need to, to continue to find power in them. A phrase can work for me for relatively long or short periods of time. Possible focus phrases include:

- I work from my highest self.
- I give myself fully to that which I am called to do.
- Always choose love.

However you choose to do it, continually cultivating and tending to your own energy and internal condition is the foundational work on which all transformational facilitation and organizational healing depends.

# Conclusion

*I am still learning — how to take joy in all the people
I am. How to use all my selves in the service of what I
believe. How to accept when I fail and rejoice when I
succeed.*

— Audre Lorde

Learning and growth come from everywhere if we allow it to
be so. This idea appears in many spiritual traditions. Buddhists
call it beginner's mind. In Jewish tradition, there is an idea
called *Hitlamdut*: learning from everything. *Hitlamdut* teaches
that when we are dying, we are still learning — learning how to
die because it's not something we've done before.

This has been my experience as a consultant: continually
learning and growing. Even when I have been in a similar
situation before, I have never been in this situation with these
people. And if I have, we are ready to evolve further because we
are back here again. I am called to deepen my connection and
commitment every day. To welcome my voices of doubt but not
let them lead the way.

Learning to be with each other more truthfully and presently,
with care and skill, is not optional. And it's not just good, sound
business practice. It is fundamental to creating a more just world.
We need tools to listen, express ourselves clearly and honestly,
dream, and create. And we need people willing to guide individuals
and groups vulnerably and powerfully in and through this work.
I hope that the resources and perspectives I have offered here will
contribute to your ability to be one of those people.

At the end of a training, Barry Oshry once said, "Now you
know what I know, AND you know everything that you know."
I wish you many blessings, much joy, and continued learning
in your work.

# Appendix: Tools and Resources

I love tools and frameworks and I can't imagine consulting without them. And it's also true that tools are just that: tools. I use them to make meaning and give structure to the work, but they are not the sole key to the magic that can happen in well-facilitated processes. They are vehicles that we animate with our presence, our care, and our intentions.

Each section of this appendix features a key set of my favorite tools and resources, many of which I have referenced earlier, some of which I developed myself. I follow these with brief descriptions of well-known tools and frameworks that are highly useful but appear in so many other articles, books, and websites that I didn't feel the need to go into detail about them. There are lots of other tools and resources that you may find helpful, and I urge you to seek them out if the ones I include here don't resonate for you or meet your specific needs. I hope that over time you will find what works for you and make it your own.

## Tools and Resources for Planning

- POP: the foundational framework for all planning.
- Strategic Moments: a useful tool for framing strategic thinking and problem solving.
- Strategy Filter: a tool for an organization or team to discern what activities they will — and won't — do.

## Tools and Resources for Navigating Conflict

- The Conflict Avoidance Escalator: a framework for understanding the consequences of conflict avoidance.

- Non-Violent Communication: a tool for deepening human communication and connection.
- DiSC: a tool for understanding team and individual behavioral styles.

## *Tools and Resources for Meetings and Decision-Making*

- Check-ins (and outs): a guide for facilitating check-ins.
- Meeting Guidelines: processes for setting group norms and expectations.
- Circle Processes: tools to structure conversations for deep listening.
- Fist to Five and Thumb Polls: tools for assessing a group's readiness to come to agreement around a particular issue.
- Deep Democracy: a methodology for facilitating groups to find real agreement grounded in exploration of seemingly opposite positions and ideas.
- Decision Matrix: a tool to determine roles in decision-making and other processes.

## *Tools and Resources for Navigating Change*

- The Wheel of Change: A framework for understanding the dimensions of change processes.
- Appreciative Inquiry: an asset-based approach for looking at systems or challenges and catalyzing change that uses what is already working within a system to address the things that are not working.
- Immunity to Change: a tool for surfacing hidden assumptions and mental models that inhibit our ability to make desired changes.

## *Tools and Resources for Understanding Systems*

- Organizational Assessment and Team Assessment Tools: a set of questions I developed for conducting an organizational or team assessment.
- Seeing Systems: a framework for understanding how power impacts organizational function and dysfunction.
- Organizational Ecosystems: a framework I developed for understanding the impact of individual, team, organizational, and societal influences on different aspects of a system.

## Tools and Resources for Planning

### *POP*

The POP framework (Purpose, Outcomes and Process) developed by Leslie Sholl Jaffee and Randall Alford is one foundational tool for every type of planning I do, from multi-year change processes to short meetings.

POP represents three sets of questions to answer, in this order, when planning:

**P**=Purpose: Why are we doing this? What is our one succinct and clear reason to do something?
**O**=Outcomes: Where do we want to be, and what do we hope to have at the end of our time together?
**P**=Process: How will we get there? What will we be doing?

I am almost evangelical in my enthusiasm to spread this framework. It makes my day when clients tell me that the question "What's our POP?" has spread throughout their organization. I know then that their meetings and processes will become more "on purpose" and hence more effective.

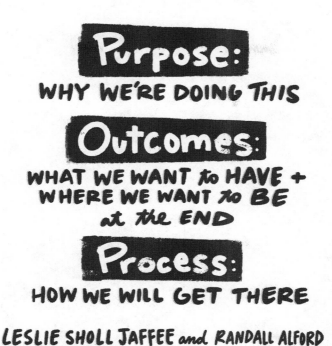

**Purpose:**
WHY WE'RE DOING THIS

**Outcomes:**
WHAT WE WANT to HAVE + WHERE WE WANT to BE at the END

**Process:**
HOW WE WILL GET THERE

**LESLIE SHOLL JAFFEE** and **RANDALL ALFORD**

*Strategic Moments: What to do when you don't know what to do...*

This simple yet profound framework comes from the Interaction Institute for Social Change. It is a cousin, perhaps even a sibling, to POP. They are not mutually exclusive and in fact are quite complementary.

IISC says that "Strategic Moments are those points in a discussion or team process when people are faced with a choice about what to do next and how to do it. The leader's job is to help navigate the group through these moments."

This framework offers three questions, which we ask in the following order (though the diagram that illustrates the framework places the third question in the middle and the second at the end):

1. *Where Are We Now?* What is true in this moment, both internally and in the world around us? What do we know, what do we believe, and what's true about who we are and our context? (first circle)
2. *Where Do We Want to Be?* What is our vision of what we want success to look like? (last circle)
3. *How Do We Get There?* What action is needed? (middle arrow)

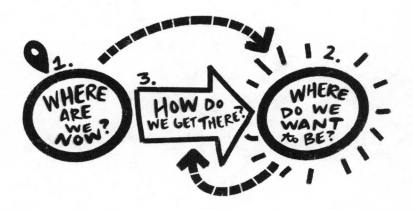

**INTERACTION INSTITUTE for SOCIAL CHANGE**

Many people skip straight to action in their work, asking only the question: What do we need to do? This framework helps us see that we make our actions strategic when we situate them within the tension between where we are now and where we want to be. We are looking for the right stretch between those two poles to create momentum for forward movement. Too much of a stretch and we break. Too little stretch and we have no dynamic tension and hence no energy for movement.

I use this framework when I am stuck in a process and don't know what to do. I ask myself or the group: "What is everything I or we know to be true right now?" When I say (or write) these truths out loud and then articulate where I or we want to be, a path forward almost always opens up.

My colleague and I were scratching our heads. The board of Animal, Vegetable, Justice (AVJ), a food and environmental justice advocacy organization, had engaged us to help them become stronger and more effective. Our initial interviews with board and key staff revealed significant tension and mistrust throughout the organization, among the board, and between the board and Betsy, the ED. Years of conflict around strategy, patterns of damaging gossip, and some earlier financial mismanagement had contributed to this moment of hurt, pain, and frustration.

We saw that the organization was at very real risk of imploding. The needs were enormous, and we didn't know where to start. It reminded me of a knotted ball of yarn: very tangled, hard to find the ends, and with the potential to make the tangle worse if we pulled in the wrong way.

Then I remembered. "This is a strategic moment!" I said. Within our anxiety, we both felt a moment of breath. We wrote down everything we knew to be true about the current situation and where we knew AVJ wanted to be. We asked ourselves the classic question that we had learned from Nonviolent Communication: What needs are currently unmet here? This revealed a wealth of insight. Throughout the system, we saw unmet needs for belonging, respect, clarity, contribution, and shared truth.

These insights enabled us to develop an iterative process that began with grounding the board in the purpose of the organization and acknowledging the truth of where they were in the current moment. We supported the board members to share their stories of what had drawn them to the organization and why it meant so much to them. We helped them tell the truth and mourn their past missteps. We worked with them to establish norms and expectations for their work and each other and create a shared vision of where they wanted to be as a board. This loosened the tightly tangled state they were in and set the stage for further planning and healing.

## Strategy Filter

I first learned about strategy filters from David La Piana's book *The Non-Profit Strategy Revolution*. They are extremely useful tools for making organizational decisions. As I use them, strategy filters can be absolute criteria, (i.e., something that MUST be true in order for the organization to take something on) and/or a set of discernment questions (i.e., questions to guide decision-making, but not absolute must-haves).

Sometimes using a filter can provide a definitive direction. Sometimes it opens awareness of issues that surround a decision, informing the conversation around difficult choices. When used consistently, strategy filters build the habit of strategic thinking throughout the organization.

I usually include a strategy filter in strategic planning as it provides excellent parameters for what the organization knows it will and won't do. We can also develop an organizational strategy filter as a free-standing tool without an accompanying strategic plan.

For a strategy filter to be successful, leaders need to model its consistent use and value the time it takes to slow down, remember to refer to it (!), and use it to examine the possibilities. This can be as simple as pulling out the filter when a decision needs to be made and running the options through it.

Strategy Filter Example
*Criteria that must be met in order to take on anything new:*

1. *Fits with our Mission, Vision, and Values.*
2. *Has impact in a particular geographical area.*
3. *Fits within current staff capacity and/or allows for additional funding and necessary infrastructure.*
4. *Directly impact the needs of a specific population.*
5. *Has partner buy-in (if we need partnership to do the work).*

*General discernment questions to ask ourselves when considering anything new:*

1. *Are we uniquely suited to do this? Can the problem or issue be solved or addressed by others?*
2. *Will we be making meaningful change? How will doing this work impact the individuals, organizations, and/or systems we care about?*
3. *What collaborations can we leverage or build to support this work?*
4. *What might we need to give up in order to do this?*

## Tools and Resources for Navigating Conflict

### *The Conflict Avoidance Escalator*
The Conflict Avoidance Escalator shows how avoiding conflict sows division, perpetuates harm, and fosters organizational dysfunction. I modeled it on William Kriedler's Conflict Escalator, which maps how conflicts go from minor to violent, and Chris Argyris' Ladder of Inference, which shows how we draw and then act upon inaccurate conclusions.

The boxes are what we experience, starting with the original event. The thought bubbles are the stories we tell ourselves based on our perceptions of what has happened. The arrows are the actions we take, or don't take, based on the conclusions we've drawn. The actions that we take escalate further misunderstanding, tension, and, eventually, loss of trust and authentic relationship.

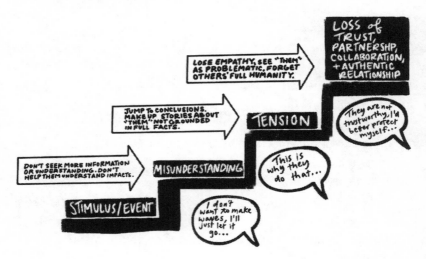

So what does this look like in practice? Let's say my co-worker doesn't get me a piece of information when they said they would. I could ask them about it (stepping off the escalator), but because I don't want to upset them or make them feel bad, I decide not to say anything. And because I haven't said anything, I don't understand why they didn't get it to me or what challenges they might be facing. We are going up the escalator!

In the absence of actual information, my brain, as all human brains do, fills in the holes with mistaken facticity. It's how our brains tend to work. We don't like uncertainty so any explanation is, in the very short term, better for us than nothing at all. It is easy for me to assume that they didn't give me the report because they don't respect me and don't value my time. My mistaken facticity is driving me further up the escalator.

Now there's tension between me and my co-worker, whether or not they (or I!) am aware of it. I don't think they respect me, so I begin to protect myself against them. I don't show them my authentic self, and I withdraw from them. I begin to see them as untrustworthy. Perhaps I imagine they don't have my best interests in mind.

At the top of the escalator, sometimes in the most subtle of ways and frequently outside of my conscious awareness, I stop seeing them as fully human. My heart closes to them and a division opens up between us. The next time I need something, I may well turn to somebody else.

Instead of going up the escalator, I could simply communicate that I didn't receive the report when I was expecting it and ask if they are having difficulties with it without blaming, shaming, or making up stories about their intentions. In so doing, I can open up to the possibility that authentic communication, with true curiosity and openness, could deepen our relationship.

When I introduce this framework, I often see knowing nods and hear murmurs of acknowledgement. *"I do this all the time!"* someone exclaimed excitedly in the middle of a recent retreat. Many of us are going quickly up this escalator many times a day.

### Non-Violent Communication (NVC)

NVC, developed by Marshall Rosenberg, offers a simple method for listening with care, expressing clearly, and bringing empathy to all interactions. NVC teaches us to connect with our own needs and desires and to listen for the needs of others underneath the words they are speaking. NVC has helped me to hone my ability to hold humans with dignity while also holding them accountable for the impact of their behaviors.

## DiSC

Organizations use a plethora of behavioral and personality assessments. For the past ten years or so, DiSC has been my favorite. It gives incredible insight into the impact of our behaviors on others and the environments we need to do our best work. I use it a lot in leadership coaching and especially love using it with teams to open dialogue about how they are working together and what they each need to do their best work as a member of that team.

## Tools and Resources for Meetings and Decision-Making

### Check-ins (and Check-outs)

Joyce Shabazz and I developed these guidelines for meeting check-ins based on the work of the wonderful colleagues and teachers we have learned with over the years.

Check-ins are one of the most important ways to welcome people into meetings and create alignment. Whether they are quick or lengthy, light or deep, they provide a chance for people to connect as human beings and transition our attention into the meeting space.

But check-ins are not a thing we do just to have done it. The goal of the check-in is to create an energetic field for the group within which we can show up and hold each other with dignity and fuller humanity. The energy of the group aligns when we hear from each other.

Although some folks who do not like process may find opening check-ins painful, I still insist on them every time. When we skip them, we miss powerful opportunities for deepening relationships and aligning with our shared purpose that can affect the results of our work together.

I always start meetings with a check-in. Period.

Factors to consider as you design check-ins include:

- **Time available:** Do you need something quick? Will allocating more time to the check-in help to achieve desired outcomes or build relationships within the group?
- **The size of the group:** The larger the group, the more time it will take.
- **The outcome you are seeking:** Are you looking for lighter or deeper connection? What do people need to be able to enter the meeting well?

It is useful to have a springboard prompt for people to speak to. Some types of prompts include:

## Topical

- In a meeting about technology you might ask for "A favorite tool or platform you use in your work."
- In a meeting about youth you might ask for "One word that would describe you as a young person."

## Quick

- A two-word check-in.
- A weather report—ask each person to describe how they are today in terms of weather.

**Light** (A light question can bring some levity to the group and help participants get to know each other better.)

- What's a favorite food?
- What's a favorite flower?
- What's a favorite song?

## Share news

- What's something that's going well?
- What's something new in your life?
- What's something you're working on that is interesting or challenging?

## Deepen interpersonal understanding

- What's something from your culture or heritage that gives you strength?
- What is the origin of your first [or last name]?
- What is a place that you just love to be?

There are many ways to determine the order in which people speak, including:

- **Go around:** Call on people to speak in the order in which they are seated or on screen.
- **Popcorn:** People speak when they are moved to speak next.
- **Volleyball:** Have each speaker choose the next person to speak when they are done. This should be done with care so as not to recreate the experience for folks of waiting to be chosen for a team in middle school.

I also invite people to go around the room at the end of each meeting to say a few words to close up our space. This might be what they are taking away, what they are committing to, a new thought or idea they had, how they are feeling in this moment, or what they will continue to think about. If time is tight, I might simply have each person share one or two words as a closing thought. A closing go-around gives energetic closure to a meeting. I want people to leave meetings as connected as possible to each other and what we've just accomplished together.

## Meeting Guidelines

Whether we call them meeting guidelines, meeting agreements, norms, or ways of being, they let everyone in a meeting know what behaviors are expected and develop an ethos of accountability to those behaviors. Guidelines help us to know how we're going to be together. This is particularly important when we are working across cultures.

Meeting guidelines can be set in advance and brought to the group or developed by the group together at the start of the meeting. This depends on the time available and how important the guidelines are to the life of the group. If it is a group that will be together over time, or needs to build trust, I like having the group develop them together. If time is limited, building trust is not necessary, or the group is large, I provide guidelines.

Regardless of how guidelines are developed, it's important that every person in the group understand and agree to them. I explicitly ask if anyone needs clarification about any of the proposed guidelines or cannot agree to them for any reason at all. Once we have addressed any questions or concerns that arise, I ask for agreement with a show of hands. We may well find ourselves straying from our guidelines, but this explicit agreement helps me and anyone else in the group to call us back to our aspirations.

It's important to use common sense in managing guidelines. Once, someone in a group proposed a guideline to "turn phones off." I asked if any of the proposed guidelines needed clarification, or if there was any reason someone wouldn't choose to agree. One person raised their hand. Their partner was nine months pregnant and could go into labor at any time. They did not turn off their phone!

Guidelines can seem like a throwaway when we toss up the usual list without much thought or investigation, letting it hang on the wall without further attention. Not useful. I try to build muscle memory for the ways a group wants to be by pointing out when they are practicing their guidelines and operating consistently with their values. I periodically remind standing groups that meet over time about their guidelines, particularly if we are about to engage with a potentially challenging topic.

The facilitator, of course, has responsibility for the success of the meeting, but so does every member of the group. Anyone can notice and speak up, without blame or shame, when the group is drifting away from their agreements or when they are doing well. All it takes is a simple "I'm noticing we're not ..." or "I'm noticing we are..."

Guidelines should be framed as actionable, doable behaviors, not abstract concepts. For example, "Practice Respect" can be difficult because that behavior can look different to different people. When someone proposes an abstract guideline, I ask them to say what it would look like and what specific behaviors we would expect of ourselves.

I like to frame guidelines in positive terms — as the actions we want to see, not the negative behaviors we don't want to see. So we might adopt "One person speaks at a time" instead of "No side conversations."

Guidelines for meetings I facilitate usually include some or all of the following (I have included the typical explanation I offer for each in italics):

- Practice deep listening. *Listening is a skill that takes a lifetime of practice. Each time we come together is a chance to practice our listening, build our capacity to pay attention, and really hear what another person is saying, with their words and with their breath.*

- Share the air. *I encourage people to share their voices and also to make sure that we share the space equitably, noticing the role that dominance and identity can play in who takes up space and who does not and making space for all voices.*
- Keep confidentiality. *Share the outcomes and learning of our time together as we have agreed but keep individual contributions and thinking in this room.*

## Meeting Evaluations

Doing an end-of-meeting evaluation allows us to learn from our process and note important issues that may still need attention. It helps both the group and the facilitators know what went well, so we can do more of it in the future, and know what could be changed, so our work can be even better next time.

Meeting evaluations can be done while we are still together or as a post-session survey. I like having groups do it together in the moment for a few reasons. First, it creates shared accountability for the work we have just done. Second, it promotes a culture and habit of giving and receiving feedback. Lastly, it's important for people to hear from each other, not just for me and my colleagues to learn from the feedback.

I like the phrasing of "pluses and wishes" rather than "positives and negatives" or "pluses and deltas" (what could be changed or different). It's much easier to say a wish, and a wish is also easier to receive than a negative or something else that might land as critical. I generally ask, "What worked about what we did? What might we have done differently? What might we do differently in the future?" I then listen to what is offered with an open heart and open ears, without defense, pride, or expectancy.

## Circle Process

Circle processes are ways to practice deep listening and build understanding among groups. They are used for restorative justice processes when harm has happened and also as a simple facilitation tool. Here I will talk about them as a facilitation tool.

Quite simply, the facilitator poses a question to a group and then the members of the group respond, going around in a virtual or actual circle. Each person in turn gets a chance to respond to the question and to listen deeply, without interruption or dialogue, to everyone else as they speak. Everyone has the right to pass and to speak later, when the circle comes back around to them or at the end of the round.

In the places where I first learned this process, including the Alternatives to Violence Project, Findhorn, and graduate school, people passed an object around the circle to indicate whose turn it was to speak. When a person was done speaking, they handed the object to the person next to them. I subsequently learned that this practice was developed by people indigenous to this land now known as North America. I understand that white people using this practice was not welcome by some Indigenous people, so I have stopped using an object during circles.

If there are a lot of people and a limited amount of time, I use a timer and give everyone the same time limit. Peggy MacIntosh, the author of *The Invisible Knapsack of White Privilege* calls this "the autocratic allocation of time for the democratic allocation of voice."

## Fist to Five and Thumb Polls

Fist to Five and thumb polls are useful, quick tools for helping groups reach agreements. They are so popular and widespread that I don't know where they came from! When a group has generated a proposal or is considering a proposal that has been brought to them, you can use these tools to gauge the level of agreement. In Fist to Five, you ask people to weigh in on the proposal with their fingers: one finger means no agreement, five means full agreement, and anything less than four fingers should be discussed. In a thumb poll, thumbs up means "I agree," thumbs down means "I don't agree," and a sideways thumb means "I'm not quite satisfied with it and want to talk more about it" or "I'm not sure." These polls can be used before and during discussion of an issue and work well in tandem with other processes, like the circle processes detailed earlier.

Neither of these tools are a vote. They are simple ways to gauge where members of a group currently stand vis-à-vis a decision. They can indicate whether or not a group is ready to make a decision and whether there is sufficient understanding and agreement on a decision.

## *Deep Democracy*

Deep Democracy is a thorough methodology with many tools and processes for helping groups make decisions and move through conflict. It was developed in highly polarized post-apartheid South Africa by Myrna and Greg Lewis, based on the work of Arnold Mindell. Deep Democracy is grounded in Jungian theory and views groups and systems as singular energetic fields rather than sets of distinct individuals. When divergent perspectives exist in groups, Deep Democracy holds that they are all pieces of the group's one collective subconscious. Deep Democracy calls positions that seem to be opposites polarities. Often polarities are seen as contradictory and competing, but Deep Democracy holds them as part of the same energetic field.

The powerful array of tools and methods that Deep Democracy offers are designed to surface and address the underlying factors and ideas that are keeping groups stuck. Working with the energetic field resonates strongly for me and my background in acupuncture. I have seen Deep Democracy processes lead to powerful breakthroughs in thinking and shifts in how groups decide to move forward.

## Decision Matrix

A decision matrix is a tool for clarifying roles and responsibilities when making decisions.

Benefits of using a decision matrix include:

- Achieving the right participation, which doesn't mean that everyone is involved in every decision but rather ensures that the right people are included
- Clearly assigning roles and responsibilities
- Promoting cross-functional collaboration by identifying relationships and expectations
- Aligning work with plans

There are many different decision matrices. Some popular versions include DARCI, MOCHA, and VARCI. I like VARCI because the roles relative to decisions are clearer to me than some of the others, but also because it's the one I learned first. I learned it from Rockwood Leadership trainer, Jose Acevedo, and it has worked for me for many, many years, so I'm continuing to stick with it.

The name of the tool is an acronym for the different roles people may play in relation to decisions or pieces of work. In this case, those roles are Veto, Accountable, Responsible, Consulted, and Informed (VARCI).

### V = Veto

Some organizations have no need for this role, but in others it is essential. The V has the ultimate authority, which means they can veto decisions made by others. The V should provide clear constraints and parameters and be kept informed as processes progress.

## A = Accountable

A's are ultimately accountable for the program or project, which includes being the designated decision-maker. They may choose to do this in consultation with R's and C's. A project can only have one A, but the A can be an individual or a group acting in concert (e.g., a board of directors).

## R = Responsible

R's carry out or share the work that the A is accountable for.

## C = Consult

C's are stakeholders with expertise, experience, and interest in the project. C's have an opportunity to be consulted and contribute to the project or decision before it is finalized. They are not decision-makers unless the A decides that their input will be the final word.

## I-Informed

I's can expect to be informed of progress and key decisions so that they can do their jobs or collaborate on a project.

To use the matrix, list the areas of work and decision-making in the left-hand column of the matrix and put the roles (VARCI) across the top. Whether a group works on this together or an individual or smaller group prepares a proposal to share with a larger team, it is important to ensure that everyone involved understands the roles and who holds them.

To pre-empt opportunities for confusion and misunderstanding, managers should continually make sure that everyone is clear on their responsibilities. The matrix should be revisited and revised as often as needed.

EXAMPLE:

| ROLES→ AREA of WORK↓ | V | A | R | C | I |
|---|---|---|---|---|---|
| HIRING STAFF | EXECUTIVE DIRECTOR (ED) | PROGRAM DIRECTOR | | ALL STAFF | ALL STAFF |
| SET HR POLICIES | | BOARD | ED | ALL STAFF | ALL STAFF |

*"It hangs right over my desk,"* my client Catalina told me about her organization's VARCI chart. *"I look at it nearly every day."*

Like all tools, VARCI only works when you use it!

## Tools and Resources for Navigating Change

### The Wheel of Change

The Wheel of Change, developed by Robert Gass, is a simple yet profound framework for understanding the dimensions in which change happens. It holds that transformation requires ongoing attention in three areas:

- *Hearts and Minds*: our attitudes, emotions, and beliefs.
- *Behaviors and Skills*: our actions, which are well known to be louder than words. (I have added "skills" to the original "behaviors," as I believe skills are important for shifting behaviors.)
- *Structures*: the systems, policies, and practices that we operate inside, which dictate our actions and behaviors.

Each of these dimensions of change makes possible the others, hence the wheel. Structures create the contexts within which we operate. Our hearts and minds drive our behaviors. Our behavior dictates what actually happens and what systems and structures we create.

Organizations can sometimes believe so strongly in one of these dimensions that they neglect the others. I've had several clients who valued hearts, minds, feelings, and relationships to the extent that they were unable to develop the systems, structures, and skills that would support accountability. Overvaluing hearts and minds can manifest as an inability to give feedback and speak truth to each other for fear of damaging relationships. It can also show up as an inability to clarify expectations, which can lead to lack of accountability and skill across the organization.

I keep the Wheel of Change in mind throughout change processes to ensure that we are continually attending to each of the dimensions as we move forward. Teaching it to clients helps them see which dimensions they rely on and which may be absent from their work.

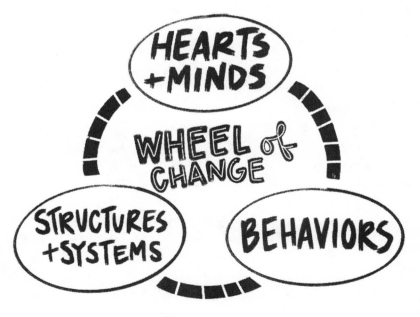

## *Appreciative Inquiry*

> *What we choose to emphasize in this complex history will determine our lives. If we see only the worst, it destroys our capacity to do something. If we remember those times and places — and there are so many — where people have behaved magnificently, this gives us the energy to act, and at least the possibility of sending this spinning top of a world in a different direction.*
>
> — Howard Zinn

Appreciative Inquiry, developed by David Cooperrider, is a methodology for approaching questions, situations, and problems from an asset-based perspective. As Einstein said, "We cannot solve our problems with the same thinking we used when we created them." Appreciative Inquiry helps us lift ourselves out of our current mindsets and transform our ways of thinking to discover new possibilities.

Central to the Appreciative Inquiry approach is telling stories grounded in what is working, even if that is just kernels and scraps. It is not about ignoring problems and pain. Rather, it is about contextualizing them in the light of what is enlivening and energizing. What we direct our attention toward is what we carry into the future. Focusing on what is working allows us to hold in relief what is not working. We can look at those things in the light and energy of what is possible, not just as deficits and deficiencies.

I weave an Appreciative Inquiry approach into almost everything I do. I have used Appreciative Inquiry as the basis for planning processes, structuring the process around lifting up what is thriving, then looking at what is not working well and what needs to shift.

I often start meetings or processes with questions about what is working and go from there. Beginning with these questions is usually energizing, but I need to be careful to frame them so that I meet people where they are. I don't want to come in all cheery and rosy when people are suffering. At the same time, I want to move the conversation toward what is life-giving. This is as much about my tone and the context I provide as the question itself. Some sample Appreciative Inquiry questions that I use to start sessions or processes include:

- What is something you value about your work here?
- What is something you're proud of that we do here?
- What is one of your favorite memories from your time here?
- What is a time when you felt really alive and on purpose in your work here?
- What about this organization attracted you? Why did you come here? Why do you stay?

## Immunity to Change

Immunity to Change, developed by Lisa Lahey and Robert Keegan, offers a radical twist on goal setting. Its four-step process helps us look beneath the barriers that keep us from reaching our goals. Through this process we surface mental models and what Keegan and Lahey call our "hidden competing commitments." These are the beliefs, rooted in mistaken facticity, that feel essential to our survival and drive our behaviors.

- *Step One: Our Improvement Goal.* This is the one significant improvement goal that would make a really big difference for us if we actually achieved it.
- *Step Two: What's in the Way?* We list all the behaviors that we do (or don't do) that get in the way of reaching our

goal. I call this the compassion part of the process. As we speak these behaviors out loud, we hold them with compassion and care, knowing that at some point they were adaptive solutions to problems. Holding them with compassion is, as Brene Brown teaches, an antidote to the shame that keeps us stuck in old patterns.

- *Step Three: Our Worries and Fears.* In this step, we list all our worries and fears about what could happen if we stopped doing the behaviors in Step Two. This leads us to our hidden competing commitment, which is our commitment to prevent our worries and fears from coming true. These "hidden" commitments drive behaviors that can be contrary to our stated desires, preventing us from reaching our goals. Uncovering them can be a game-changing experience.
- *Step Four: Our Assumptions.* We look at the assumptions underlying our worries and fears and see that while outside of our awareness we believe them to be true, when we speak them out loud, we can see that they are not actually true, or at least are not as true as we believed them to be. Once we see this, we can work to break the hold they have on our beliefs. Once our belief systems shift, we find that the behaviors they have been driving can also shift.

I have used Immunity to Change for both individual and team development. It's not a casual tool to use, as it asks participants to go to a vulnerable place. For many of my clients it has provided life-changing insight. Others are not ready or interested in doing that kind of self-discovery. When I think it could be useful, I offer it to clients. I tell them what it entails and let them decide if they are interested in that kind of exploration.

# Tools and Resources for Understanding Systems

## *Organizational and Team Assessment Tools*

These assessments tools can be found in my paper, *Where Does it Hurt? Health and Disharmony in Organizational Ecosystems.* You can use the questions to create a survey, to guide focus groups, or as the basis for interviews to gather perspectives on the condition of the organization or team you are working with.

### Organizational Assessment Tool

- Do staff have a clear shared sense of the purpose of this organization?
- What are the primary goals of the organization? How were these determined? How are they evaluated? How are programs and operations aligned with larger goals?
- What are the values of this organization? How do these values manifest in daily operations? Are these values shared widely within the organization? Are they taken seriously?
- What is the organizational structure? Are the appropriate processes and people in the right places to accomplish organizational goals? Are the lines of accountability clear?
- How are resources managed? Does resource allocation match the organization's espoused goals?
- How are decisions made? Are the people affected by decisions able to contribute their wisdom and insights?
- What words would people use to describe the organizational culture?
- How does the organization address racism and systemic oppression?
- How does the organization handle conflict and address harm?

- What types of behaviors does this organization value most? How does it reward these behaviors?
- How does the organization support staff well-being?
- What mechanisms are in place to assure accountability? How is good performance rewarded and poor performance addressed?
- How does the organization promote and reward learning, innovation and continual growth and improvement?

I prefer qualitative questions to quantitative ones, but it can also be helpful to ask an organization or team to rate itself on a scale in indicators of organizational effectiveness. Such indicators might include:

- Our mission and purpose is clear.
- Our mission and purpose is widely understood throughout the organization.
- Our values and foundational ideas are clear.
- Our values and foundational ideas are widely understood throughout the organization.
- Our operations and actions as an organization are consistent with our values.
- The identities and cultures of staff are valued and honored.
- We have a shared analysis of systemic oppressions.
- We have clear and effective processes for conflict resolution.
- We have clear goals as an organization.
- Our goals are widely understood throughout the organization.
- Individual staff have clear goals that align with larger organizational goals.
- We have mechanisms to understand and evaluate our progress.
- Our organizational structure is effective.

- Our resources are well managed.
- Our decision-making processes are clear.
- Our decision-making processes are fair.
- Our organizational culture is welcoming and supports staff to do their best work.

It is also important to look at governance. Some questions to ask include:

- Does the governance of the organization mirror the organization's values? Too often, justice-oriented organizations replicate dominant, top-down leadership with their boards. This can look like a board not reflecting the communities they serve, making decisions without the input and wisdom of staff, and not operating internally with the culture of generation and creativity that the organization might promote.
- Is the governance effective? Does the board support the needs of leadership? Do they help to ensure that the organization has the resources it needs and that those resources are used wisely? Does it help to further the mission and work of the organization?

### Team Assessment Tool

- What is the purpose of this team? Is this understanding shared by all team members?
- Does this team deliver on its goals and commitments? If not, why not?
- What is the quality of relationships between team members? Is there trust?
- Do team members feel they can rely on each other?
- Do team members see team meetings as productive and meaningful?

- Is there a shared understanding of team members' roles and responsibilities?
- How are decisions made? Are processes and roles clear to all team members?
- What is the quality of team communication, both formal and informal?
  ○ How is information shared between team members?
  ○ Do team members give and receive all the information they need?
  ○ Do team members find their communications with one another satisfying, or do they avoid communication?
- How does the team handle conflict and disagreement?
- How is difference in identity and culture handled within the team?
- How does the team reflect on its work and continually learn and improve together?

*Where Does it Hurt? Health and Disharmony in Organizational Ecosystems* is a free download available at http://docs.just-works.com/Where-Does-It-Hurt.pdf.

### Seeing Systems

Many people have written about the relationships between individuals and systems in the context of organizational dysfunction and change. Barry Oshry's simple and elegant insights into organizations and power have been the most helpful for me.

Oshry posits that outside of our awareness and intention, human systems will usually stratify in predictable ways around perceived or positional power. When we are not aware of the system dynamics, most people will behave in predictable and often ineffectual ways based on our perceptions of where we are in the system.

Oshry's framework breaks systems into four spaces people occupy:

- Top Space: People who have the ultimate responsibility for the system
- Bottoms Space: People who deliver or produce the goods or services of the system
- Middles Space: People who manage the Bottoms on behalf of the Tops
- Customers: People who benefit from the goods or services produced by the system

One of the great beauties of this framework is that we can all be in each of these spaces depending upon our context, sometimes shifting within the same day. They are not who we are; we occupy them positionally. I may be in Top Space in my department, but in Middle Space relative to the Executive Director or CEO, Customer when I go out for lunch in the middle of the day, and in Bottom Space if there is an organizational retreat with managers and the board of directors.

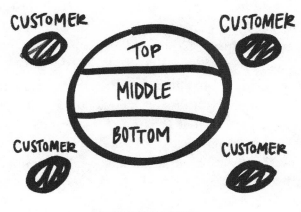

Oshry teaches that rather than us playing these roles, the roles play us. We think we are seeing clearly, but we are actually seeing through the very limited lens of our current role. Even though we are moving between spaces, when we are in a role, that is what we see. We can easily lose empathy and find ourselves othering people in the rest of the system.

Oshry details predictable ways that most people will behave when we are in these spaces:

- People in Top Space will take on all the responsibility, disempower others, and devalue the contributions, and sometimes even the humanity, of Bottoms
- People in Bottom Space will feel disengaged, disempowered, and vulnerable. They will hold the system itself or the Tops responsible. Bottoms often find community and/or disenfranchisement in their mutual bottom-ness
- People in Middle Space will be torn between the demands of the Tops and the demands of the Bottoms
- Customers will feel righteously screwed by a system that just doesn't pay attention to their needs

These predictable responses bring us out of our real power and authentic relationship with other people in the system. Oshry teaches that unless we are mindful of the typical system dynamics at work in our contexts, our actions will perpetuate separation and hence oppression. The good news is that when we understand these system dynamics, we can make choices to own our power and agency.

Both personally and professionally, this framework has dramatically shifted how I understand human systems. I have witnessed it in almost every system I have worked with, even those that reject hierarchy or strive for flat or distributed leadership.

The subtitle of Oshry's important book *Seeing Systems* is *Unlocking the Mysteries of Organizational Life*. It does indeed offer a clear window into our chaotic worlds, as well as language to help call people to a bigger perspective when they get caught up in the miasma of power dynamics. More than one client has told me excitedly "I stayed up all night reading *Seeing Systems!*"

Oshry has developed several experiential workshops to lift the veil of how system dynamics play out in real time and build a common awareness and language for systems thinking. Some of these workshops can be done within organizations.

## Organizational Ecosystems

In *Where Does it Hurt: Health and Disharmony in Organizational Ecosystems*, I introduced a holistic framework for looking at organizations as living ecosystems comprised of four concentric layers: Individual, Team, Organizational and Societal.

The Individual Layer is at the center of the ecosystem. It is made up of us, the people whose energy and effort is the lifeblood of an organization. Organizations are, ultimately, collections of infinitely complex individuals, with all the gifts and baggage we bring.

The second layer is the Team Layer. This is where individuals meet. It contains interpersonal relationships, group dynamics, and work processes. If the Individual Layer is where we are in our relationship with ourselves, the Team Layer is made up of the ways we are in relationship with each other, both interpersonally and in our work processes.

Even in organizations that consist of only one team, the Team Layer is distinct from the third layer, the Organizational Layer. The Organizational Layer contains the organization's Guiding Ideas (mission, vision, and values), strategy, structures, resources, infrastructure and policies.

The Organizational Layer, along with the most exterior layer, the Societal Layer, provides the context for teams, individuals, and their work. The Societal Layer contains the factors that are outside of the actual organizational entity but still influence and inform the organization's work. These factors include laws, mores, culture, and history.

Energy flows dynamically between these layers, whose effectiveness depends on the flow and quality of that energy. What happens in one layer impacts the other layers. For example, if we are thinking about complications in our team, we don't always think about the influence each individual member has on the team, nor how the organization's policies and values impact team dynamics. It is rarer still for people to consider how societal influences, such as racism and other oppressions, affect the dynamics of a team.

This model allows us to look at where disharmonies in organizations are occurring and the ways in which the different layers of the ecosystem are impacting each other. We can then design interventions to address root causes, not just symptoms.

As an acupuncturist, I could just treat the symptoms of a client's headache and often this would bring relief. But if they had chronic headaches, providing symptomatic relief was a start but not a cure. To truly support healing, I needed to look holistically within and outside of the body. What life habits (diet, etc.) might be contributing to the headaches? And within the body itself, what other systems might be impacting the flow of energy to the head?

This framework helps me see where the roots of disharmonies may actually lie so that we can transform them.

BUSINESS
BOOKS

## Business Books

Business Books publishes practical guides
and insightful non-fiction for beginners and professionals.
Covering aspects from management skills, leadership and
organizational change to positive work environments, career
coaching and self-care for managers, our books are a valuable
addition to those working in the world of business.

## 15 Ways to Own Your Future
Take Control of Your Destiny in Business
and in Life
Michael Khouri
A 15-point blueprint for creating better collaboration,
enjoyment, and success in business and in life.
Paperback: 978-1-78535-300-0 ebook: 978-1-78535-301-7

## The Common Excuses of the Comfortable Compromiser
Understanding Why People Oppose
Your Great Idea
Matt Crossman
Comfortable compromisers block the way of anyone trying to
change anything. This is your guide to their common excuses.
Paperback: 978-1-78099-595-3 ebook: 978-1-78099-596-0

## The Failing Logic of Money
Duane Mullin
Money is wasteful and cruel, causes war, crime and
dysfunctional feudalism. Humankind needs happiness, peace
and abundance. So banish money and use technology and
knowledge to rid the world of war, crime and poverty.
Paperback: 978-1-84694-259-4 ebook: 978-1-84694-888-6

## Mastering the Mommy Track
Juggling Career and Kids in Uncertain Times
Erin Flynn Jay
*Mastering the Mommy Track* tells the stories of everyday
working mothers, the challenges they
have faced, and lessons learned.
Paperback: 978-1-78099-123-8 ebook: 978-1-78099-124-5

### Modern Day Selling
Unlocking Your Hidden Potential
Brian Barfield
Learn how to reconnect sales associates with customers
and unlock hidden sales potential.
Paperback: 978-1-78099-457-4 ebook: 978-1-78099-458-1

### The Most Creative, Escape the Ordinary,
### Excel at Public Speaking Book Ever
All the Help You Will Ever Need in Giving
a Speech
Philip Theibert
The 'everything you need to give an outstanding speech'
book, complete with original material
written by a professional speechwriter.
Paperback: 978-1-78099-672-1 ebook: 978-1-78099-673-8

### On Business And For Pleasure
A Self-Study Workbook for Advanced Business English
Michael Berman
This workbook includes enjoyable challenges and has been
designed to help students with the English they need for work.
Paperback: 978-1-84694-304-1

### Small Change, Big Deal
Money as if People Mattered
Jennifer Kavanagh
Money is about relationships: between individuals and
between communities. Small is still beautiful, as peer
lending model, microcredit, shows.

Readers of ebooks can buy or view any of these bestsellers
by clicking on the live link in the title. Most titles
are published in paperback and as an ebook.
Paperbacks are available in traditional bookshops.
Both print and ebook formats are available online.
Find more titles and sign up to our readers' newsletter at:
collectiveinkbusiness-books.com/
Facebook: facebook.com/CINonFiction/
Twitter: @CINonFiction